D0327059

Cinderland

MONROEVILLE PUBLIC LIBRA

4000 Gateway Campus Blvc

Monroeville, PA 15146

Cinderland

A memoir

Amy Jo Burns

MONROEVILLE PUBLIC

JUN 0 1 2015

LIBRARY

BEACON PRESS, BOSTON

Beacon Press
Boston, Massachusetts
www.beacon.org

Beacon Press books
are published under the auspices of
the Unitarian Universalist Association of Congregations.

© 2014 by Amy Jo Burns
All rights reserved
Printed in the United States of America

17 16 15 14   8 7 6 5 4 3 2 1

This book is printed on acid-free paper that meets the uncoated paper ANSI/NISO
specifications for permanence as revised in 1992.

Text design by Ruth Maassen

Many dates, names, places, and other identifying characteristics of people mentioned in
this work have been changed to protect their identities. The communal voice is not
intended to presume upon the memories and experiences of others but to reflect the
shared nature of the event itself, as the author remembers it.

Library of Congress Cataloging-in-Publication Data
Burns, Amy Jo
  Cinderland : a memoir / by Amy Jo Burns.
    pages cm
  ISBN 978-0-8070-3703-4 (hardback : alkaline paper) — ISBN 978-0-8070-3704-1
(ebook) 1. Burns, Amy Jo, 1981—Childhood and youth. 2. Teenage girls—
Pennsylvania—Biography. 3. Child sexual abuse—Pennsylvania. 4. Girls—Abuse of—
Pennsylvania. 5. Truthfulness and falsehood—Social aspects. 6. Truthfulness and
falsehood—Psychological aspects. 7. Community life—Pennsylvania—History—20th
century. 8. Pennsylvania—Social conditions—20th century. 9. Pennsylvania—Biography.
I. Title.
  CT275.B78594A3 2014
  616.85'8360092—dc23
  [B]
                        2014009918

For the seven;
and for all the others, too.

Contents

Prologue

BY THE TIME THE POLICE entered our houses uninvited throughout the fall of 1991, our mothers had already commanded each of us to tell the truth about Howard Lotte, and we'd already decided to lie. It was too impossible for anyone to conceive, even those of us who had sat with Mr. Lotte and his feckless hands through seasons of week-night piano lessons, that such a man could commit something so unholy, even if he was a little bit fat. Everyone in Mercury knew which girls had already snitched. We saw what it had cost them. The best hope for the rest of us, we thought then, was to remain anonymous until winter arrived and all the talk turned to idle chatter before it disappeared altogether.

But the gossip about Mr. Lotte would not be squelched, and so the police launched a formal investigation to put the rumors to rest. Making a uniform circuit around town, the squad stopped at the homes of each of Mr. Lotte's peach-faced, preteen protégés. Some of the homes were split level and some were Victorian, but none of them were trailers. Mr. Lotte didn't seem to take on *those* kinds of girls. Anyone who was anyone took lessons from Mr. Lotte—if you were female, of course.

When each of our turns came to be questioned, the lies spilled out so easily we suspected they'd been planted long ago. There were few girls—seven, to be exact—bold enough to tell the truth, but their soft-voiced protests were almost drowned out by those of us unable to defy a town rallying behind one of its own. Though we were just ten, eleven, twelve years old, it became quite clear that men like Mr. Lotte secured a kind of protection that girls like us never could.

The police supplied the questions, and we offered the answers we thought they wanted to hear. Like a swooping she-owl, our voices raised into an echoing chorus as mothers drew the shades for the night and the distant five o'clock bell signaled a shift change at the mill.

Did he put his hands on you?

No, Officer. No, he didn't. No no no no no.

The sound found its way to the woods by the edge of the school yard where an old basketball hoop had been torn from the ground and laid prone some time ago, the same spot where lovesick boys dared to press their burning palms against a girl's. Then the sound moved toward the courthouse at the center of town where Mr. Lotte wouldn't get the opportunity to appear before a jury of his peers. Our voices only weakened once they reached Mercury's city limits, where the highway cut us off from the rest of the world.

Now the town itself haunts us more than Mr. Lotte, even more than our own lies. It seems a story like this couldn't happen anywhere but Mercury, a place that had become its own needy planet, a town we loved for its empty houses, abandoned buildings, and vacant lots. The people of Mercury liked their trucks, their Iron City beer, and the stench of burning leaves. They knew how to work with their hands—how to sew a quilt, how to fix a carburetor, how to patch a roof. They knew how to wait out a tough winter.

Together we all lived in the afterlife of a city that was once a titan. A very long time ago, Andrew Carnegie evangelized the steel gospel. He followed a simple formula: Contain the coal. Set it on fire. Strip away the impurities. Dispose of the slag.

This was how a legion of unstoppable steel rods was sired. But then came the Steel Apocalypse, and Pittsburgh's satellite cities didn't all become ghost towns only because many people had no choice but to stay. Instead, the loss of our lifeblood slowed everything to a pace that was barely detectable, and the era of waking sleep began.

Workers who used to pull twelve-hour shifts in the mill at Cooper Bessemer Steel in the next town over now had nowhere to go. The roads once clogged with commuters became open highways. Mostly, people just sat. And the children, of whom we were some, watched. We remember now how people around town used to float through the amniotic air. Pumping gas. Ordering pizza. Waiting in line at the drive-through ATM. Pushing the shopping cart through the dog food aisle at Rip's Sunrise Market. Taking long pauses in the middle of sentences. Not bothering to finish them. They used to think nothing could surprise them any more until Mr. Lotte proved them wrong. He proved us *all* wrong.

Who are we? We are the girls who lied about Mr. Lotte when others told the truth and most of Mercury hated them for it. We performed for a fickle crowd and lost ourselves in the charade. From the moment we chose to protect a criminal, we also chose to forget everything that had happened. It was our best chance for survival. Even so, our lives were never the same. Our town was never the same.

Our memories threaten to make a scandal of us, so we keep them to ourselves. We still remain in disguise (even from each other), but there's one thing we know. Our Sunday school teachers had always taught us that an honest answer was like a kiss on the lips, and we were not the kissing kind.

PART I

Spotlight

Prisoner's Dilemma

THE SUMMER I TURNED FOURTEEN, I got caught looking for love on Whore Hill.

It had been four years since the start of Mr. Lotte's investigation, three years since I made myself forget it ever happened, and over ten years since the steel industry fell and broke everyone's hearts. In a town full of highways and unemployed mill workers, there was only one way to get out. The kids on the hill saw each other as escape routes, and so the games between us began.

It was the summer of 1995, and it turned out to be the summer of rain. Throughout the month of June, the worst hurricane season in decades slammed the Atlantic Coast with water, the constant downpours a complement to the postindustrial sobriety that had washed over western Pennsylvania. Would-be days of sun and chlorine were supplanted by sluggish hours spent counting the seconds that split lightning from thunder.

The glut of dreary June days sequestered the kids around town to their bedrooms, and collective lethargy set in. Like a propagating yawn, we were suckers for herd behavior. If one member of the herd bolted, we all bolted. If one member stopped to take a piss, we all pissed. Our silent pact was simple:

I. Ain't. Doin.' Nothin'.

As the rain fell, securing a backlog of paying work for my father's small roofing business, the neighborhood kids couldn't be bothered to leave their own houses. It was as if we'd settled into the crease of a communal couch and couldn't summon the energy to get up. The pervasion

of sloth limited most of our conversations that summer to some deriva-
tive of the following:

"Hey," one of us would say.
"Hey," the other would answer.
"What are you doing later?"
"Eh. I ain't doin' nothin'. You?"
"Ain't doin' nothin'."
"*Ain't* ain't a word, dumb ass."

When the hurricanes tapered in late June, we reemerged, slovenly
and pale, and swarmed the public pool in Silver Pulley Park. All the
regulars (or the "pool rats," as we were known) came out for the first
swimmable day of the summer. I felt damp grass on my feet as the fellow members of my brood and I staked out the highest point of land
by the steel fence, a territory the lifeguards had coined "Whore Hill."
A congress of available girls was always in session, though never without a gaggle of boys in tow. Girls in Mercury struggled to befriend
each other, except as accomplices in crimes of love. Two binary max-
ims had been woven into our collective moral fiber: boys would be
boys, and girls would be trouble.

We'd grown up learning that the steel industry was our town's long-
dead lover, and we sat in the soot of what had once been a fiery affair.
On a map, a cross marked the spot where Route 17, running north to
south, impaled Route 44, stretching east to west. This was Mercury: an
intersection, a meeting place standing halfway between Pittsburgh and
Erie. There was iron in the water, coal in the ground. You could hold
your breath and drive all the way through town without needing to exhale. At night, the courthouse clock tower in the town square gleamed
like a lonely jewel in a rusted crown. On Mercury's outskirts, Whore
Hill overlooked the pool, the parking lot, and the metal jungle gym
where kids liked to smoke. Despite the rain, parched grass covered most
of the hill. Beneath a peaked sky, my comrades Nora, Jill, Becca, and I

arranged our towels in a neat row on the rise of the hill. We leaned back, relishing the glint of the meager sun on the tops of our pasty thighs. If I squinted, I could see the distant tree leaves shaking in the wind.

Jill, a math whiz better known for her body's lusty curves, leafed through the pages of a paperback horror novel. We often traded and discussed these books at length, the plot twists, the evil twins, the red herrings. We dared the books to shock us. Becca switched on a portable radio, and Blind Melon's distorted guitar notes wafted through the air. The red curls dangling from her pony tail lolled back and forth as she nodded to the music.

"That's my *song*," I said.

"Every song is your song," someone answered as Becca turned up the volume.

In the far corner of the parking lot, a handful of men spread hot pitch along half of the road that circled the park. These men had once spent their summers dawdling at the pool. That was how it was around here. You were the shit until one day you weren't. We watched them push a smoking wheelbarrow full of gravel from one end to the other. Their bare backs glistened with sweat like a pop can in the sun as they raked the hot tar into flat lines.

Nora, my closest confidante, handed me a cherry lollipop and I passed her the suntan lotion, SPF 8. We'd been inseparable since my childhood friend Carly and her family had left town three years ago after Mr. Lotte's investigation ended. It was big news when people left Mercury. "They'll be back," people in town liked to say, and often they were proved right. But Carly was gone for good.

Some of Lotte's other girls—though no one called them that—dispersed through the crowd that day at the pool. Layne Richter laughed with her friends while taking a quiz in a teen magazine. An athlete, Layne was lithe, strong, and fearless. Another girl named Aria Tierney manned the snack shop, which operated out of one of the utility closets. Aria ran it when her older brother Simon left to attend basketball or soccer practice, and she sold ice-cold Milky Ways out of a freezer while an old box fan shot hot gusts of air out the door. I admired Aria from a distance for the same reason I admired Layne. Fear had never led them astray.

Though Nora and I had both taken piano lessons from Mr. Lotte, we'd never spoken of him despite all the other secrets we shared. Speaking his name was a slur against the town, and we knew enough to ration our indiscretions. Slanting back on her towel, Nora swept her black hair into a ponytail as we watched a few boys race toward the water and dive beneath its still surface. Nora's red bikini was dry, as was my navy one-piece. I'd never gathered the nerve to wear a bikini. I was known around town for what I wouldn't reveal, especially if someone came searching for it.

The frigid water only tempted brash boys looking to flaunt their *cojones* for an audience. With our cunning disguised in comatose stares, Nora and I had perfected the appearance of reluctant spectators. Secretly ambitious, we had plans. Plans to make something of ourselves. Plans to get out of this town.

But for the moment, we sighed. We yawned. We tried to appear on the brink of sleep so if a boy happened to drip water on us, we could feign shock. Propped on our elbows with our dazed gazes sheathed in wide sunglasses, we started to shop for boys.

There were two kinds of boys that we browsed from our perch at the top of the hill. The first was the "puppy jock," a guy who was crisp and athletic, deeply tan, with very white teeth. He was a challenge—a little bit out of your league, and that's how you liked it. He looked like a brightly colored Popsicle in his neon swimming trunks, jaunting across the slabs of concrete with his friends. He would take off his shirt in all kinds of weather. While it was true his sense of humor flirted with the idiotic, when winter came he'd wear his lady's cheerleader pin on his jacket. He wasn't afraid to tell her he loved her, and she never doubted he meant it.

This was the kind of boy we liked to watch on the high dive, his body arcing with perfection as he leapt from the board, a fine specimen to examine as he penetrated the water. He'd be loyal, not to mention helpful around the house. Should his beloved need to take a trip to Rip's Sunrise Market, he wouldn't hesitate to step in and say, "Let me bag your groceries."

The second kind of guy hanging around the pool didn't throw his money or his services around. We'd spot him slouching outside the fence or down by the jungle gym, but he never came inside. His accessories: clove cigarettes and a tiny stud earring in his left ear. For lunch, he drank a cold can of Hawaiian Punch that no one saw him purchase. He didn't need to eat. He owned a large selection of metal band T-shirts, every one of them faded black.

These two kinds of boys—separated by an old, rusty fence—never mixed, but the girls volleyed back and forth between them. There were three kinds of girls playing the game around the pool: those who advertised their participation, those who appeared to be oblivious to the game, and those who acted as if they were superior to it.

Around here, a girl could not escape her reputation. Instead, she had to determine what it would be. Prude. Slut. Bitch. Snitch. I preferred the kind of reputation earned for what I didn't do, rather than what I did. Accordingly, I designed a triad of rules for protection:

1. No random hookups.
2. No sex.
3. No second chances.

I tried. In one year's time, two rules I would keep; one I would break.

When I was still young enough to think pools were just for swimming and friends were made for keeping, the water seemed worth the fear I once had for it. Back then, Carly was still around, and I visited her one afternoon to go swimming in her pool. Floating in an inner tube, I leaned back and felt the sun on my face. I remember thinking I'd found Mercury's only paradise. Even at seven years old, the summer had a way of making me infatuated with the only home I'd ever known.

Without warning, an unseen force thrust me from the water. The inner tube upended and trapped me beneath it. I heard the water crash and saw the foam of the waves before I went under. Once submerged, everything fell silent. I grasped upward and flailed, but the bulging plastic had me pinned. My eyes started to play tricks on me. Aquamarine spots spread the length of the pool floor, like a leopard's fur coat.

Supine, I lay there for a minute, not yet drowning. I could see Carly's tan legs kicking in the distance—but toward me or away from me? There I was, trapped in a paradise-turned-prison, and all I could focus on was the miracle of Carly's rootlessness in an underwater realm where some things just didn't float. Her kicking couldn't have lasted more than a few seconds. I couldn't have known then I was looking through a watery crystal ball into her future, into the way her family would have to leave town—on their feet and in a hurry.

I blinked and the sun shot through the water. The inner tube popped up, and I was free. Gasping, I sprang to the surface. Carly's mother was the first thing I saw at the pool ledge, on hands and knees, her expression fixed with terror. She slumped with relief when she saw me. Her son, two years younger than me but twice my size, had overturned the inner tube and used his own weight to hold me down. "I was just playing," he said as his mother fished me out. It was the first time I was conscious of being completely overpowered, and I hated it.

After that, my mother committed her summer afternoons to taking my older sister, my younger brother, and me to the Silver Pulley pool where I first caught a glimpse of the older girls on the hill. My mother sat with her paperback book but hardly ever read it, instead prepared to pounce if any of the older bullies started splashing one of her children. That was my mother: vigilant watchtower, faithful companion, the first person I ever loved. When we tried to cajole her into the water, she claimed it had never been quite warm enough in the small Maine town where she grew up for her to get the hang of swimming. Sometimes we'd convince her to slip in a foot, an ankle, or perhaps her torso. Mostly, she contented herself by watching us from the base of the hill, and I'd hang back in the shallow end testing the water with my toes, while Julia and Seth charged ahead.

Years of swimming lessons helped lessen my phobia, but my final showdown with the water occurred when I was ten. I thought it was the day I'd conquer the last of my fears because I didn't know what was coming. It was the summer right before the rumors about Mr. Lotte started to surface and everything in Mercury changed. That summer afternoon, my father had brought my sister Julia and me to our lesson to see us jump off the diving board. I had yet to attempt it, and I perched on the edge of the board for ten minutes, peering over the lip into the turquoise below.

My father watched us from the top of Whore Hill on the other side of the fence. He leaned against it, his fingers slung against the metal. His skin was a deep tan from all the late afternoons he'd spent roofing that summer. Waiting on the board's cliff, I stared at him, and then the water. I wanted so much to impress him, this man I loved who wasn't afraid of anything. When fear overtook me, I crept back toward the ladder and climbed down the rungs. I looked once more at my dad and shook my head, and he waved me toward him.

I ran up the hill to where he waited at the fence. Shielded by a pair of sunglasses and his roofing hat, I couldn't gauge his expression.

"Why won't you jump?" he asked.

I slouched. "I'm afraid."

"Ah," he said, scratching his forehead with the bill of his hat. "So this is a test."

"A test?"

"A test. Is fear going to rule you?"

I didn't answer. My father had a way of cutting to the heart of things.

"Amy," he said. "You can do this."

"I can't."

He crouched, leveling his eyes with mine. "If you jump off that diving board, I'll give you fifty dollars."

"Fifty dollars?"

He nodded. My back straightened. I'd never seen a fifty-dollar bill before. The thought enticed me, but not as much as my father did. He had more faith in me than I had in myself, and that was worth more than all the fortune I could imagine.

I turned and ran back to the diving board. My hands shook as I grasped the ladder. Again, I paused at the board's edge, fear fastening me to it. *Is fear going to rule you?*, my father had asked me. *No*, I told myself. *No.* Closing my eyes, I pried one foot from the board. Then I stepped off the edge and fell, splitting open the surface of the water below. When I resurfaced, the sound of my father clapping echoed against the barren hill.

A few days later, my father presented me with a smooth fifty-dollar bill. I couldn't bring myself to spend it. I kept it safe in the back left corner of the desk drawer in the room I shared with my sister. I took it out once every few weeks to look at it before returning the bill to its hiding spot. With time, it crumpled and folded in on itself.

It remained in the drawer for years as Julia and Seth grew bored with going to the pool, and then a few years later, it was still in the drawer when I outgrew my regular trips to the pool as well. It had become a talisman, worth more to me as a possession than a payment. Just a few months after I jumped off the diving board for the first time, I'd lie to the police to save myself from being shunned by the town I loved. There it was—my bravest accomplishment palm-to-palm with what would become my deepest regret.

By three o'clock in the afternoon, the Silver Pulley pool teemed with people. A few boys had plopped their towels around us before tearing down the hill to jump into the water. I watched them splash each other. They cast an occasional glance our way, and we answered with intermittent nods. A few other boys had passed the concrete line, trolling the grassy incline and pawning back rubs. The girls on the hill popped their knees to the side and tossed their hair. They'd circled my troop a few times because we'd scored the prime part of the hill right by the fence. With brown hair and a petite build, I might not have been much of a threat, but I made up for what I lacked in sex appeal with shrewdness: I knew enough to arrive early and claim my territory. One of the blonds eyed us as she ran her fingers beneath the elastic of her bikini bottom: a ceremonial flare of her starting gun. The games were about to begin.

Becca and Jill lay on their stomachs, absently flipping through fashion magazines to disguise their whispers about a few prospects gathered by the high dive. The hopeful back-rubber arrived at our camp, looking optimistic about his chances. Nora decided to bite, and he sidled up behind her. From the concrete, a few female lifeguards eyed us as they played their own standard move—a reproachful headshake chased with a whisper. I could almost make out the words on their lips: w-h-o-r-e-h-i-l-l.

Primed to maintain appearances, we pretended to play for thrill, but much more was at stake. It was our version of the "prisoner's dilemma," that story economists use to explain how people are prone to operate in self-interest. Two conspiratorial criminals are kept in separate interrogation rooms, and each is provided an incentive to rat the other out. Silence is the only way to ensure mutual protection, but in the end, the police usually convince them to betray each other. The game becomes about winning, and the path to freedom is blocked by those you call friends. If you want out, you'll have to railroad your accomplices on your way out the door.

This wasn't about love. It wasn't about sex. It was about fear. We had time to burn, yet a subversive sensation warned us that time had already expired. In this town, bad boys were quick to become young fathers, and good boys, soldiers. We were aging fast, and we knew it.

At the edge of the pool, a lean, tanned boy in orange swim trunks hoisted himself out of the water. I knew who he was. His name was Pete. Athlete. Italian. Smart. A challenge—one year older and a bit out of my league. He caught my eye and puffed out his chest. Chlorinated water dripped from the hem of his trunks. I slipped him a half smile, then yawned. He smiled wide. My cheeks felt hot. He turned, getting a running start before jackknifing into the water.

I preferred this kind of performance over conversation. The fewer words the better. Too much talking and one of us would betray ourselves. I didn't dare divulge how afraid I was that I'd never get out of this town. That I'd never get to ride in a limousine. That I'd never get any farther west than Cleveland, Ohio. That I'd never do anything but listen to the merciless sound of time passing away. *Tock tock tock tock.*

Once I started talking, I wouldn't be able to stop myself. So come on, I'd say to him. Tell me what you know. Show me something. Teach me something. Please. I don't want to end up pissing my life away. You think we can get out of this town? You got what it takes? Prove it. 'Cause if I end up working the night shift at Rip's Sunrise Market when I'm thirty-five and got three kids and a mortgage on a trailer, I swear to God, I will kill myself. So you got what it takes? Prove it. I ain't got all day, so prove it, Stallion. Prove it.

♪

Allow us—Mercury's unknown legion of liars—to introduce you to another kind of prisoner's dilemma. It's the summer of 1991, Monday, 6:25 p.m. Or maybe it's Thursday afternoon at a quarter to five. No one knows Mr. Lotte's master schedule apart from his wife. We wait our turn for our lessons in the dark of his garage, hearing only the faint tap of piano keys signaling to us from the other side of the basement door. If we press our ears against it, we can hear the metronome tick.

On the other side of the wall, one of us sits on the bench in front of the piano with Mr. Lotte to our left. Before each lesson begins, his first task is to separate us from our sisters, if we have them. Upstairs with his wife, each sister will wait her turn, and then we'll switch. Sometimes, Mrs. Lotte lets us pick what television show we'd like to watch while we wait.

Mr. Lotte sits while we play. He never stands. He turns pages, he keeps the beat, and some days like today, we play together. We follow the sheet music by the feeble glow of the single lamp on top of the piano. We play the right hand; he plays the left. We lag, urging our fingers to find the right notes. His thick thumb is more than twice the size of ours.

Soon, this man will divide the town in two: those who believe in his innocence, and those who do not. Soon, he'll claim conspiracy. Defamation. Lies. He'll claim girls like Carly, Layne, and Aria are liars who want to make a criminal of him. Soon we'll have to make a choice to lie or tell the truth. If we are prisoners who want out of our own jail cells, should we pledge allegiance to a fellow girl or the man who has seized the heart of Mercury?

For now, Mr. Lotte forgives our erratic rhythms, and patiently he waits for us to catch up. Two rhythms, off-kilter, the treble a half step behind the bass. One of us plays with spastic, dissonant tones, the other with low, practiced hums of constant echo. An uneven whole, yet still we play.

This is the antecedent from which all else stems, the moment before any wrong has been done. It's almost pretty in a naïve sort of way, which is the only way a girl can be pretty around here. Everything in our small-town world has a metronomic rhythm to it, as if we're listening to our own lives from the other side of a thick door. *Tock tock tock tock.* The biggest thing we have to worry about is our monthly appointment at Dr. Shaffer's office to get our braces tightened. Even from the orthodontist's waiting room we can hear it, the blissful metronomia of our own existence, pausing there like we must pause in Mr. Lotte's garage before our lessons. We spend so much of our short, little lives waiting for something to happen. Time eats away at itself as we listen to the orthodontist drilling in an unseen room while Pam the receptionist answers the phone.

"Good morning, Dr. Shaffer's office, Pam speaking."
Drill buzz drill

"Good morning, Dr. Shaffer's office, Pam speaking."
Drill buzz drill

All we can think while we listen is how Pam's vertical bangs look like they're running away from the rest of her face. We think it's funny as we turn the pages of the *Highlights* magazine Pam thinks we still enjoy reading.

When we're not at the orthodontist's office or piano lessons, we can be found down at Silver Pulley Park until sunset. During the first pitch of a crowded little league game when the umpire, "Low Ball Bill," calls yet another strike and the fans boo, there we are, nursing our Blow Pops, scouting out our crushes, and popping tar bubbles with our toes. Or maybe we're down the hill at the pool, leaping off the diving board for the very first time. We're just girls, for now, and we have no need to hide. We have no reason to suspect that soon we'll have to armor our hearts with plates of steel.

Hide and Seek

EVEN THE MOST STEEL-HEARTED GIRLS can find themselves falling in love once in a while, especially in the fooling dark. The first time Pete and I spoke, we played hide-and-seek at nightfall. We called it Spotlight, and we let ourselves pretend danger awaited us under a sheath of bright stars hanging in a threadbare sky.

Our town looked its best in shades of blue, the dark mending our daytime ailments—rust spots, for-sale signs, empty gravel lots. Streets and houses were swept with shadow; one bled into the next. The point of the game was not finding or being found. It was about getting lost with someone, rediscovering a landscape so familiar in daylight. We only needed one flashlight to play, a sole, thin blade of light to slice through the dark. The game itself a welcome deceiver, Spotlight ransomed the mythic from the mundane.

A few nights after the rain had cleared, the pool rats met up at the house of a kid named Foss, not far from the elementary school. Foss was one of Pete's best friends; Pete had many. His friendships seemed sturdier than my own, long-lasting without threat of jealousy or betrayal. I wondered how he'd managed to come by them in a town like ours.

Foss had a good neighborhood to play in, a quiet street lined with old trees. Though I hadn't played Spotlight with the pool rats before, I was well practiced. I played it every year at Pure Heart Presbyterian's church camp. I'd played it in the woods. I'd even played it in winter. I knew how to capture myself inside the darkest of spaces and wait there with my eyes closed tight.

Nobody who played Spotlight ever wanted to be found. Someone waiting alone in the dark was a culprit or a goner, but when a boy—a strapping boy—said to a girl under the cover of night, *Come on, I know a place*, she wouldn't be able to catch her breath for the romance of it. Romance was knowing you were alive in a town everyone else thought was dead, knowing no one would come looking for you, knowing they'd stopped looking long ago.

Becca and Jill had already entangled themselves romantically for the summer, and they wouldn't dare leave the partner-selection process to chance. After snatching up two of Pete's other friends named Sam and Kev, Nora paired up with Foss, both of them preferring the "are they or aren't they" status over an affirmative attachment to someone of the opposite sex. So that left me and Pete—and Charlie, tall and forlorn, who was "it" for the first round and went by himself.

The best Spotlight games occurred in pitch black, so in the moments before dusk shifted to darkness, we waited. See us before we became what we'd always be known as in Mercury: Becca and Sam, eventual cheerleader and star quarterback, respectively, sitting on the curb, fingers entwined. Sam still with braces. Jill and Kev, both lanky and auburn-haired, future small-town basketball marvels. A snapshot of Pete, just before his own athletic prowess arrived—his feet skittered against the dark asphalt as he waited next to me. I tried to dampen my own excitement, my green eyes recently unveiled from a pair of glasses. Here, as daylight lingered, we all thought only of consummating our infatuation.

On either side of the street, old houses stood over us, filled with people who were still known by what they used to be. That quarterback from the year we made it all the way to the state championship. The girl who always flew at the top of the cheerleader's pyramid. If they watched us from their darkened windows, we didn't see them. They might as well have been ghosts peering at us through the opposite side of the same mirror.

———

Once we were alone, I found the danger I thought I was seeking: the pull of a boy's body to a girl's, the friction when they touch for the first time. I led the way through the dark in search of a place to hide. I could feel Pete right behind me—the chill of late evening, the heat of another body closing in. I said nothing. I had been primed long ago for silent performances.

Danger. What a rare thing to behold in this sleeping-beauty town. That's what I told myself, at least. Danger, I thought, was its most thrilling when moonlighting as innocence. But Pete was about to invite me into a new kind of thrill I hadn't known I wanted. We had reached the stretch of power lines by the farthest boundary point when he first spoke.

"Come on," he said, grabbing my wrist. "I know a place."

He led me back toward Foss's lawn to a house right next door where the blur of the family room television flashed like distant lightning on the grass.

"What are you doing?" I hissed. "We'll get caught here for sure."

"Shh."

I followed Pete to the corner of the lot where a large pine tree stood. He lifted the bottom-most branch before disappearing beneath it.

"No one will find us here," he said.

Once I climbed in after him, an old, familiar Mercury silence set in. This silence had been a shape-shifter as long as I'd known it; the quiet that lulled me to sleep was the same force that had seized my voice so long ago. Just a prick of the finger, someone's hand at your throat—those invisible wounds that never make a sound, and yet their silence spins at the heart of the universe.

"Hey," Pete said.

"Hey."

"You know Trent Reznor, right?"

"Come on," I said. "Everyone knows Trent Reznor."

Trent Reznor, the lead musician of the rock band Nine Inch Nails, had grown up in Mercury. About fifteen years older than we were, he left town after he graduated. He'd actually done what all of us dreamed of. He got out.

"Amy." Pete said my name. "You have to listen to their music. It'll change your life."

"I will." My heart stirred as the night's stillness hung above us. "I promise."

Pete shifted in the dark. "I want to get out of here. Like Trent did."

The words pierced me. "Me, too."

In saying three small words—I want out—it was as if Pete and I had just grabbed hands and leapt off a cliff. The secret to survival in Mercury was never admitting you wanted to leave so that if you never did, you could claim you never wanted out in the first place. *Not forgetting where you came from*, people called it. Those words hung like an anvil around my neck. I didn't *want* to want to leave, just like I didn't *want* to want Pete. The risk of disappointment was far too great, the promise of sacrifice too firm. And yet, a fire still burned deep down inside me. It was the wanting itself that revealed signs of life.

Pete's confession made me want to see him again and again—tonight, tomorrow night, and every night after. I had the strange sensation that somehow Pete knew me the best out of anyone, and he didn't really know me at all.

For the rest of the summer, I couldn't wait for sunset. I loved the feeling of lying next to someone underneath a sky of stars, whispering but not touching. I didn't care if other girls were baring their bodies in empty baseball dugouts and pickup trucks. I was getting high on the quiet risk of secret truths, even while I kept my darkest secret hidden.

The dark would always draw the young in Mercury, and the young would always long to slice it open with a naked flame. In August, one of my friends, Sidney, threw a housewarming party that gave us the chance to play with fire. Sid's parents had just purchased a new mass-manufactured house that arrived one day on the bed of a truck, prebuilt. Their old trailer had been pushed to the edge of their property where it sat in the shadow of an old swing set and a riding lawn mower, now another Mercury relic that remained long after its expiration date.

It was a cool evening, a dark blue sky with a cord of velvet smoke curling through it. Sid was an expert at stoking fires, and this party's bonfire was one to remember. Like a fat little kid, the bigger it got, the more we fed it. My friends and I sat dangerously close to the flames, but fire wasn't something we feared. If a sleeve or a shoelace ignited, it would burn in the open air until someone put it out. And then it would be a story to tell.

Pete had first kissed me on a night like this one. We'd slipped outside the Spotlight boundary lines and walked through the woods to a clearing that met up with the back part of a shopping plaza where Rip's Sunrise Market and Coyote's Pizza set up shop. At that time of night, the lot was deserted. Dirty pennies littered the ground.

In the distant light from the lampposts, I could see Pete in muted colors, the crimson of his shiny basketball shorts, the bright ivory of his teeth, the deep black of his hair. His tan hand grabbed hold of my pale wrist.

"Hey," he said.

"Hey."

My hand tingled beneath his fingers. The sensation Pete gave me was like a roller coaster mounting its first hill, the kind that inspires a rush of bravery on its quicksilver descent toward the earth.

Across the street at the local ice cream shop, a pink-and-yellow neon light flickered like the flash of a camera. The light sounded a faint buzz, as if it was just about to go out. That night, as we fell outside the boundary lines, it felt all right to be young and stuck in a dead zone, a place outsiders claimed had "never recovered" from its losses. The last thing I saw was the dark curtain of Pete's eyelashes as he closed his eyes and leaned toward me.

On the night of Sid's party, Pete and I shared a stump by the fire. Streaks of orange rose before us, pawing at an endless expanse of black sky. My eyes stung from the smoke, but I couldn't stop looking at the flames. A discarded plastic cup melted in the heat. My friends piled on the kindling, tossing old furniture, dust rags, and Styrofoam plates—things that had no place in Sid's new house—into the fire.

It was a night like any other. Foss kept burning his hot dogs. Jill and Kev were fighting. Sam tossed a football in the air. Nora attracted a flock of boys. Some kid ate all the cheese curls. Time passed, first slow, then quick. There was silence, always the silence. Somebody made a joke, a few people laughed. Everyone watched the fire breed.

As summer ended, the rain returned. No more hide-and-seek at nightfall, no more secrets shared beneath the quiet trees. Instead I listened to Pete's Nine Inch Nails album like he'd asked me to. I'd never heard anything like it, and the music both frightened and seduced me. At times, Trent Reznor's voice was low, melodic. And then the next second, it changed to a series of hoarse screams. I'd heard that the whole record was meant to represent a character's psychological devolution, a downward spiral. Even at a low volume, the music refused to be ignored.

Trent's song "Closer" stood apart from all the others. Its hook had a mod, electronic feel. The beat was slow. Controlled. The probing lyrics about sex and God shot through me as one word took center stage: *fuck*.

Once a long time ago—before Carly left, before Mr. Lotte—she and I shared a hushed conversation about sex.

"Sex is bad," she whispered to me while we were sitting in the back of a church. "It's in the Bible."

"Oh," I said.

"I'm never having sex," Carly told me. "Not even when I'm married."

It was strange the way Carly appeared in my thoughts, as if an evanescent fog dissipated for a moment, revealing her fixed place in my memory before the fog rushed in again. It was the only way I could have her now, the only way any of Lotte's girls could have each other. Honesty had to be surrendered or apologized for, so terrible was the consequence of telling the truth.

The way Trent Reznor's mouth formed the word made me think he wanted his audience to feel every letter. I imagined his likeness as he said it. His teeth dug into his thrusting bottom lip for the "F." The "U," his mouth opened in invitation. And the strong click of the "CK" at the back of his throat echoed like the cocking of a gun. The word was not just a verb or an action. It was an emotion. A mood. A statement. Every time he said it, I felt the sound shake my sternum. In Mercury, good girls didn't say "fuck."

Our initiation into the sorority of good girls in Mercury begins long before we're called upon to perform any good-girlish duties. That way, when the time comes, we won't have to be called upon at all. We learn by watching all the other virtuous beauties who come before us, skinny little things who cheer with the rest of the squad and smile for the camera and bite their nails in secret.

We're taught that a good girl must be careful who she's seen with. A good girl seen with the wrong kind of boy can adulterate her virginal status, turning her not into a "bad girl"—because that title suggests a kind of sexuality that makes everyone a bit uncomfortable—but into a "girl who got herself into trouble." Once a girl gets herself into trouble, her good-girl crown has been cracked and can never be repaired. The best she can hope to become is a "girl who made some mistakes," or even worse, a "girl who is still figuring it out." If you're a girl who is still figuring it out, you may as well give up now and claim your stool down at the bar on the outskirts of town because that's where you're going to end up in five years anyway. There's never much talk about the boys themselves who are responsible for leading good girls astray. Boys will be boys, and girls ought to know better.

Speaking of boys, there are three black boys in town, and they're handsome like you've never seen. Good boys, too—strong hands and worn letter jackets—but you'll find them walking the road alone at night, always alone, especially when it's cold. These aren't summer's kind of boys. They're down at the park, they're behind the elementary school, they're not looking for a ride.

Every girl's daddy waits in line to slap these boys on the back after they win Friday night's game, but don't you forget. He'd push the same kid off his porch if he dared show interest in his daughter. *Don't you come around here*, the grown man would tell him, his face veiled by the screen door. He won't say it isn't right, or that it's not our way. He likes the kid too much to admit the truth.

So every good daughter pines in private. Her daddy never says, "He just ain't fit for you, honey," because she already knows not to ask. She thinks she's not confused about where real danger hides.

A good girl knows she can avoid danger by keeping her mouth shut, and not just about Mr. Lotte, though that time is coming fast. Mrs. Lotte has her own harmless, meant-for-nothing secrets, and we don't mind keeping them. In the summer of 1991, we spend rotating afternoons with Mrs. Lotte, eyeing her as she sits erect on the couch, her hand squeezing the television remote. Summertime typically means the end of school year piano lessons, but as good girls, we are always eager to improve.

We wait in the velour recliner, and the backs of our legs start to sweat. Their sweltering living room sags with sour air. On the television, we see a man with black jeans and a brown mullet clutching the bow of a ship in the middle of a severe thunderstorm. He screams into the waves. His name is John Black.

When the show goes to commercial, Mrs. Lotte's body slackens and she collapses against the cushion. After a few ads for detergent and local grocery stores, an image of an hourglass appears on the screen and a voice says, "Stay tuned for the second half of *Days of Our Lives.*"

As the scenes intertwine, we bite the bottoms of our lips and scoot forward in the armchair. Incipient fascination swells in our chests. Conspicuous clues reveal where evil lurks: in minor chords, behind thick mustaches and well-trimmed beards, between shipping crates in abandoned shipyards. In the final scene, as John Black plants himself at the bow of that cursed ship, defying the storm's attempts to rock him, the soft underbelly notes of a girl's version of the theme to the musical *Cats* waft up from the basement.

At 1:59 p.m., the credits roll. We sink back in our cushions and exhale. A secret has passed between us. Our mothers wouldn't like knowing we were watching this smut, but shouldn't Mrs. Lotte be allowed this single indulgence? She is always so kind and, dare we say, oblivious to her husband's basement behavior. From afternoon until night, her house teems with young girls always playing "Hot Cross Buns" and chromatic scales and the same opening run of notes to "The Entertainer." Doesn't she deserve this one little vice? Besides, one good girl should always assist another, and we can tell that Mrs. Lotte must have been a good girl back in her day, from the tight curls of her at-home perm and the white sneakers she wears with her pantsuit on her way to work.

Later, when the time comes for Mrs. Lotte to testify on her husband's behalf, she'll lament the past:

> Our house was always filled with music. We had a number of two-student families. While one was taking his or her lesson, the other student was welcomed to spend time in our living room doing homework, watching TV, or perhaps even chatting with me. I'm one that's very friendly to all of the students. As I look back now, I see how trivial many of those things were.

Good girls don't just do as they're told. We never *need* to be told. It's acceptable for a good girl to lie, especially in the interest of protecting someone else. We can be trusted with secrets. We know that bodies aren't the riskiest things to bare—secrets are. When we realize that sometimes it's as easy as saying nothing at all, the initiation is complete.

Emerge

IF SUMMERS IN MERCURY were a dream, in fall, time was wide awake. Freshman year began with finding a way into the town's choreography—the bowing of a league of football players as the band played "The Star Spangled Banner" on a Friday night, the flash of brittle leaves catching fire on the outskirts of town, the crowning of a new homecoming queen on the fifty-yard line in early October before the cold set in. I took my place with the rest of the band fronts on the football field during halftime of every home game, the stadium our autumnal theater. Young girls like me also became members of the *corps de ballet*, practicing for our coming moment when we'd rise to take the lead role in an entire town's performance.

Most of Mercury spent the morning after a big Friday night home game nursing their football hangovers, but I reserved the first part of each weekend for what I loved most. Every Saturday morning, my father drove me to ballet lessons in Juniper, a town half an hour away. We always stopped for doughnuts. My father knew those city streets so well he could have navigated them in his sleep. The Burns family had lived in the valleys of Pittsburgh since the time when Andrew Carnegie was still just a messenger boy.

Almost a hundred and fifty years later, I had my ballet lesson in a sleeping city. Full-length mirrors dressed the far wall of the dance studio so the students could monitor their own progress at the barre, which, for the time being, was a row of metal folding chairs. The building's owners were waiting to accrue enough cash to install an actual wooden rod. But still, on Saturday mornings, the other students and I danced for the row of slender mirrors, the forgotten industrial cityscape yawning at our backs.

Juniper was a bankrupt city, once bloated by the success and breadth of Juniper Steel. The city had been in mourning since the steel mills closed about ten years before in the late 1980s and still hoped for them to return, an Appalachian Miss Havisham, tattered and waiting for someone who would never show.

My ballet teacher Martine began each lesson with *pliés* and then moved into the *port de bras*. Slowly, my body warmed and the tightness melted. I'd never been flexible; my body held a tension that never seemed to relent except for the moments I practiced ballet. I didn't mind the pressure. It was the fighter in me, and I relied on it. In the colder months, my fingers and forearms cast a wan, bluish tint against my black leotard. Even when my core began to sweat, my fingers remained slow to react. But in ballet, this delayed movement was beautiful—*ritardando*, a slowing down. My fingers, like pale, breeze-blown ribbons, knew how to trail the path of my body.

During the center work in the middle of the room, I relished the thump of my feet beating together before landing on the floor and the way the studio blurred as I pirouetted across the room, zoning in on my mark. I liked to choose small items like a window latch, an abandoned, errant nail in the wall, the folded hands of a mother watching in the corner of the room. As I turned, these small things became my anchor.

In ballet, my body was my own. My fingers were celebrated when limp, rather than urged into action. They did not march; they floated. They did not shout; they spoke. They did not pound; they breathed.

Every Saturday, I shed more than sweat on the studio floor. I surrendered the outer selves I kept polished for the rest of Mercury to see, the prize-pony version of myself that I paraded around town. The straight-A student. The dancer at the end of the kick line on the football field. The girl who could keep a secret. What remained at the end of the hour revealed an inner heat, the heart of my dampened flame that would not die.

Ballet was my vice, but at some point it would not be enough. I'd need some other fix, like Mrs. Lotte needed her afternoon soap operas or Martine, her cigarettes. I once witnessed her smoke a Virginia Slim on the floor of the dance studio kitchen. Just eight years old, I spied her from the crevice between the door and the wall minutes before ballet class was scheduled to begin. She lay flat on her back, her head propped against the cupboard beneath the sink. The tile on the floor was gray, her spandex was gray, her hair was gray, her teeth were gray. Gray smoke lifted from gray ash. Just a small hint of orange burned at the end of the filter. Sometimes I wondered if this was what we feared most in Mercury: a moment of spark, a lifetime of cinders.

At the barre, my fingers were slow, seconds behind the mind, and yet they arrived on time. "The hand does not yet know the body has fallen," Martine told us from the front of the studio. "Let it drift behind you like a feather."

My initiation as a pretty young thing in the imaginary wealth of Mercury's social fabric would not be complete without a costume ball, and homecoming in Mercury was an event not to be missed. Held each year in the school cafeteria at the height of football season, homecoming was the small-town girl's cotillion, a way to announce one's own arrival.

The night of the dance, the pool rats—dressed in neckties and taffeta—stopped by the park where we'd spent so many summer afternoons. We wanted to take pictures in the gazebo by the lake. Pete's father drove us in his maroon Silhouette. The sun set quicker than we'd anticipated; the October days were growing short. Our jackets lay in a heap against the gazebo railing. Waiting in the dark, we appeared only in the flash of the camera. My bare, pale shoulder parting the night. Pete's black hair blending into the clear sky, his fingers tightly clasped behind his back. The bright snap of the camera washing our skin, the cold air fixing our smiles into half-moons.

This was romance: not the dance, not the corsage, not the crisp, black suit or the party dress. Romance was driving on a highway overpass, sitting in a dusky backseat, looking out the window. Picture yourself standing at the bridge covered in graffiti, peering over as the cars whoosh beneath, yelling into the wind with someone standing next to you. To mix a typical Saturday evening with high heels so later you can remind yourself what it felt like to be young.

Later, we had dinner in a darkened room of a smoky restaurant. Eight of us crammed at a small table, we tried to relax.

"Homecoming is lame," someone said.

"Fer rill," said someone else.

Foss cracked a few jokes. We used forks and knives. I took my shoes off beneath the table.

At the dance, we watched the newly crowned homecoming king extend his hand to the queen, dressed in a tiara and a sash, as they took the floor for their solo dance. This was every girl's dream: to emerge as prima ballerina. For the first time, I witnessed this ritual that had existed before my father went to high school in Mercury, the heartbeat of our town, the power it had to silence a room.

Pete and I had spent an entire summer running from the spotlight, but after I felt the hot glow of Friday night lights in Mercury, I thought I needed another halo to get me through the winter. When football season fizzled, I took my virgin dive beneath small-town stage lights. In November, the choir department held open auditions for the school musical, *Anything Goes*. Set aboard a ship crossing the Atlantic, the play oozed with manufactured drama. With stowaways, impostors, and love triangles, *Anything Goes* was the best way to wait out the coming cold.

A portrait of my rookie audition: a girl in jeans and a zip-up hoodie, nerves palpable, fingernails bit. I climbed onto the stage and popped in a tape recording of my sister playing "On My Own" from

Les Miserables on the electric keyboard. Unlike me, she still played the piano. Julia had always loved music as much as I loved to dance, and nothing would keep her from it.

Before my audition started, I stuffed my hands in my pockets.

"What part are you auditioning for?" the choir director asked.

"I'll take whatever you give me," I answered.

I lifted my chin and pressed my shoulders back as my ballet teacher Martine had taught me. Her best advice: "Don't let them see you sweat."

After pressing play on the choir department stereo, I planted myself in the middle of the stage that hadn't been renovated since my father stood on it at his own high school graduation. The piano notes crackled as they wafted out from the boom box. I squinted at the light box at the back of the auditorium for the length of my minute-and-a-half performance, my voice cracking on the high notes. I winced. Polite applause followed. I would take it.

Illusion always blooms best in winter. In the first month of musical rehearsals, the cast was given a single stage direction: "Act like you've got money." We did, and the ruses started to snowball. Pete had been cast as a sailor, and I had been cast as a rich passenger on the ship. The two of us imagined our own secret storyline—a rich, young, parentless heiress falls for a rough-and-tumble seaman who is forbidden to fraternize with the female passengers. Drama ensues.

Ignoring each other onstage had the opposite effect when we left it. In the darkened backstage wings, Pete and I kissed with my back flat against a cement wall.

"This is no time to be subtle," the director had said.

There was nothing subtle about the ways in which I fooled myself. I couldn't see how much I needed an artifice—a play, a performance, even a boy—to shield me from what was real. Fear *was* ruling me, as my father had once warned me against. I was bold with no risk, dressing

myself in pearls and fingering fake cigarettes. Inside, I told myself I was
still innocent.

⌐

Innocence can never be overrated—it's the small-town girl's currency,
and who among us doesn't want to be rich? If you know what's good
for you, you'll realize it's better *not* to know what you don't know, and
to unknow what you already do.

Here's what we won't admit we know:

In the summer of 1991, the chill of fall weather arrives before it's
due. Our town is wrenched from its summertime reverie by the sound
of insistent knocking on Mr. Lotte's door. Of course we aren't there to
hear it—we're likely sitting down to dinner with our families, or taking our bikes for one more spin around the neighborhood, or devouring the final pages of Christopher Pike's latest tale of horror—but the
stories find a life of their own as one hungry mouth feeds them to
another. The taste is so strong we could swear we witnessed it ourselves.

"I know what you did," says the angry visitor when Mr. Lotte greets
him. "I know what you did to my daughter, and I'm calling the police."

The visitor is Mr. Tierney, and he is angry because his daughter
Aria came home crying from her weekly piano lesson. The day after
she tells her parents that Mr. Lotte slipped his hand up her shirt while
she practiced playing the theme to *The Young and the Restless*, Mr.
Tierney speeds across town and bangs his fist against the piano teacher's front door.

Is this really how it happened? Probably not, since it reads like a
perfectly plotted scene from an episode of Mrs. Lotte's soaps. But the
event itself isn't nearly as important as the accounts given of it. You
can get away with just about anything if you punctuate your story by
shrugging and saying, "It's just what I *heard*," as if the rumor you're
spreading is an old dryer sheet stuck to your pants that common de-
corum insists you discharge. After all, isn't Mrs. Henderson down at
the library the most reliable person you know? She wouldn't hurt a fly,

for Pete's sake, and our mothers heard this straight from her mouth. Or what about Bill who packs our groceries down at Rip's Sunrise Market? Someone who nestles every carton of eggs in its own brown paper bag is incapable of spreading falsehood. The people of Mercury guarantee it.

Everyone around town knows Mr. Tierney. He's good with his hands, and he can be counted on to referee an afternoon soccer game as well as serve as a makeshift usher on Sunday morning if the need should arise. His son Simon is bound to make the varsity basketball team by the time he's a sophomore. No one would dare question Mr. Tierney's integrity. It's his daughter the town isn't so sure about.

How did Mr. Lotte respond to Aria's father's claims? That part of the story is rather murky. Decades later, we can't help but wonder if Mr. Lotte knew the jig was up when he opened the door and saw the expression on Mr. Tierney's face. If, even just for a moment, he considered the meager benefits of honesty before proffering an outraged denial.

But for the time being, no one seems to care much about his response at all. Instead, the spotlight is thrust on a flock of young girls who are just learning to play the piano under Mr. Lotte's careful tutelage. The benefit of being a girl is that no one expects much from you aside from a few graceful performances now and then, and as the summer comes to a close, the curtain rises. An entire town holds its breath as one question scorches its collective mind.

Which of these girls will find her voice next?

Figurante

IN THE YEARS AFTER Mr. Lotte's scandal, I welcomed the way life in Mercury could so easily become a charade. Pageantry, as I came to think of it, promised safety among my intimates. *I* would determine what others saw when they regarded me. And yet it felt as if I'd stolen away on the ship of someone else's life, estranged from who I once was. Only one tonic could sate my stowaway heart more than a charade, and that was a charade with an audience. With an audience, a lie was no longer deceitful. An audience turned a *lie* into a *performance*. And a musical? Every small town loved a good musical. Like this:

On the opening night of *Anything Goes*, an appetent crowd shoved into the lit auditorium to hunt for a good seat. During daylight, the theater stayed cool and ghostly, a forgotten space where kids escaped to steal kisses. At night, the temperature spiked as the bodies packed themselves around center stage. During a cold winter, it was the only spot in Mercury that gave off any heat.

Behind the stage curtain, the cast rustled around. We heard the crowd's murmurs, and our own anticipation mounted. To think—at this moment all of Mercury was spinning around us, waiting for us to appear. Our audience needed a performance as much as we needed to perform, and as a town, we'd never felt so complete.

Opening Scene. From backstage, Nora, Pete, and I spied the yellow spotlights pushing through cracks in the curtain. My sister Julia, acting as debutante Hope Harcourt, wafted in from stage right with her fiancé, a man named Evelyn who wouldn't be her fiancé after the play's denouement. Crooner Reno Sweeney appeared with her floozy band of Angels: Virtue, Chastity, Charity, Purity. These girls knew enough about the world to pretend to be naïve.

Spotlight. When the light first hit me, I became better than myself, larger than this town, truer than my lies. Nora and I arrived from stage right, whispering our fake secrets. We were two rich, young coquettes, but it wasn't having money that gave us the thrill. The high came from not needing it, not needing anything more than each other. We wore those roles as easily as the faux stoles at our necks—look first, and you'd see an accessory. Look closer, and you'd find protection. Closer still, you'd uncover our disguise.

Pete stepped on stage in a sailor suit and hat, swiping his broom back and forth. Nora and I mounted the stairs to the upper deck where the docks of Manhattan stood at our backs. We looked out into the audience, which doubled as the Atlantic Ocean. We stared into their shadowed expanse, the people of Mercury who lived and swam in deep water.

Subplot. My coy, theatrical analogue faded as I floated down the steps and then made my exit on stage left. Pete was waiting for me in the dark. Here it was, that hidden part of me that was so hungry, so impossible to satisfy. Pete wrapped his fingers around my wrist and pulled me behind the staging area into a thin tunnel cordoned off with a thick black curtain. A bunch of prop crates were stacked by the wall. It was black as pitch there, darker than any night of Spotlight, any basement kept in isolation. Pete gently pushed me against the crates. He threaded his fingers at the base of my back, right below the band of my dancer's tights. He ran his nose along the line of my jaw.

I heard my cue and rushed back onstage to meet Becca by the base of the steps. Over and over, the two of us performed the magic trick of speaking without words. She showed off the veil on her pillbox hat, and I fawned over her long string of plastic pearls. I twirled in the dowdy floral dress that I fished out of a Salvation Army bin. At the front of the stage, Hope Harcourt's secret love schemed to find a place to hide away.

I exited. In the dark between shafts of stage light, Pete ran the tips of his fingers up the back of my arm. The shock was electric. We said nothing and let our bodies speak.

I entered again, and Pete followed close behind. He swabbed the deck. I climbed the stairs and played with my pearls. He wiped down a porthole while I gossiped with the extras.

Offstage again, my back was flush against the crates. Pete kissed my cheek, the ridge beneath my chin. His thumbs pressed lightly into my rib cage. The eyeliner and mascara made his dark eyes pop even more in the dark. Virtue, one of the Angels, had helped him apply it. When Pete's lips finally clung to mine, I opened my eyes.

My kisses with Pete were chaste but not cleansing, a portal but not a destination. I craved those moments, those kisses, when I was thrust between light and its absence, between private moments and public shows. It seemed the only true measure of myself I could conjure—a girl who was the sum of her parts but not a whole, a girl whose hidden appetites became the maw that fed her outward persona. I could only transform into the *figurante* in the limelight because of the human I became in the dark.

"All ashore who's going ashore! All ashore who's going ashore!"

That was our cue for the "Bon Voyage" scene. At the last moment before stepping into the light, my fingers slipped from Pete's. He joined the rest of the sailors and I took my place next to Nora at the top of the stairwell.

Plot Twist. We sang. *Bon Voyage, New York City.* Pete marched to the front of the stage with the other sailors. The six of them stood in a line. For the song's coda, the sailors weaved themselves among the Angels. Virtue wrapped her arm through Pete's and squeezed, pressing the profile of her curvy body against his. I smiled and sang with my mouth wide open, but my eyes tracked the cradle of her hips. She and Pete liked to flirt with the reality of their onstage aliases, and consumed by the bloom of my own counterfeit self, I had let them.

Virtue's white denim shorts glowed beneath the lights. Her stomach was flat, a perfect, round belly button peeking out from the top of her waistband. A soft line ran down the length of her torso from between her breasts to her belly button, and it was so smooth she could roll a quarter down it. She cocked her hips toward Pete and his eyes meditated too long on the virtues of her body. Watching the two of them exposed a lie I wanted to believe about secrets—that I was the only one keeping them.

Bon Voyage. The entire cast raised their right hands and waved at the make-believe people standing on the docks of Manhattan. In those final, ephemeral chords, I couldn't determine what it was I wanted so badly. Did I want someone to help me forget what I'd hidden—not just about Lotte, but about this town, about what it means to be a quiet girl—or did I wish I'd told my worst secrets to Pete, to someone, to everyone?

The song ended, the crowd cheered, and the stage went black. Perhaps it was already too late to save myself from becoming just another girl in Mercury.

In the final scene of *Anything Goes*, the entire cast crowded the stage for a wedding about to be interrupted. We all attended the event in our best estimation of appropriate wedding attire for a boat: hats with wide brims, fake fur to stave off the chill, our fictional family heirlooms (rhinestone necklaces bought at Claire's, gold chains and pins from Sears). My sister, as Hope Harcourt, trudged into the light from stage right in a yellowed wedding gown that was two sizes too big. It belonged to one of the cast member's grandmas. Her netted veil was torn. She clutched a fake bouquet of daisies with nylon petals and plastic stems. The scene carried on more like a funeral than a marriage ceremony. Our somber faces remained stoic as the organ piped out a run of minor chords.

In just a few moments, after the vicar finished his long-winded speech, giving sufficient time for suspense to mount, Hope's secret love would burst in and proclaim that his boss made a business deal that nullified the need for Hope and Evelyn to marry. Evelyn would reveal his affair with Reno Sweeney. The Angels would coo. The wedding guests would gasp and then rejoice. We'd belt out the closing chorus of *Anything Goes* before hitting our final poses and the applause would douse us.

But first, from my mark in the back, I could see most of the cast, fifty chins all pointed toward the priest. After two hours of performing beneath hot lights, the thick, drugstore foundation caked on all our faces started to mix with sweat and slipped down our temples. It lingered along the ridges of our jaws. The stiff white collars of men's dress shirts started to soften and yellow at the creases. I looked down at my own outfit, a plaid dress that, when inspected, revealed how badly the fabric was pilling. From a distance, we were elegant. Cloche hats. Velour clutches. Herringbone blazers and skirts. Up close, we were fraying at the seams.

The actress who played Hope Harcourt's mother poised herself as if listening to a death fugue. The tight French twist in her dyed blond hair was too fancy for any other place she frequented, and the matted fur slung around her neck was secured with a fake gold brooch. The faded black skirts, the snagged pantyhose mended with hairspray, the thin-soled, white-washed shoes. Even the portholes, the brooms, the purser's list of passengers. Impostors, all of them. The purser's clipboard supposedly had the ship's manifest on it, but it was nothing more than a blank sheet of paper. Soon, we'd mourn our loss, but not because the play was dead. We'd mourn because it had never lived.

On the final night of the performance, we didn't have to fake the closing scene's sober sentiment. Since rehearsals first began, we'd dreaded the disappearance of the spotlight. This play wasn't just something to do to pass the cold winter months. It wasn't just another show. It was another life.

As with the two performances before it, after the last bow of the last show, the audience would applaud. Some would stand, some would whistle. The houselights would come up. The curtain would be drawn. The play's leads would get bouquets. The cast members would change their clothes.

They'd throw their costumes into a bin bound for the Salvation Army. After the last person left, the auditorium lights would go out. Folded programs would be left in the aisles. No one in the audience would realize that the *SS American* never actually made it to London.

Flash forward. Ten years from now, half of us will be married, many to each other. The play will become "that thing I once did." Most of the Angels will become housewives. Becca will be pursuing her principal's certificate. Nora will be running a nonprofit out of state. Pete will get an excellent job in sales. I won't have spoken to Nora or Pete in over five years.

Some of the boys will enlist. Some of the women will become very good cooks. Many of the cast members will attend Saturday night drag races on the outskirts of town, just as they did when they were teenagers. They'll sign their kids up for Little League. They'll take them to the pool. They'll wonder where the time went. Some will achieve what they set out to: they will be teachers, coaches, parents, small business owners. One will open the hair salon she always hoped she would. One or two will survive four-wheeler accidents. Some will forget to buckle their seatbelts.

Some will stay and wish they'd left. Others will leave and wish they'd stayed. I will always be looking back.

♪

It should come as no surprise that the plotline with Howard Lotte is rather musical in its execution. Every small town loves a good musical, after all.

Everyone knows the middle-aged sixth-grade teacher who gives piano lessons in the brown basement of his white house. We've seen him sporting his brown beard on walks through town with his white-sneakered wife. We've seen him every May on the day of his annual recital when he turns the pages for his students as we play the songs we've practiced all year. We've seen him each August on the first day of school, standing outside his sixth-grade classroom door as children rush inside.

Who doesn't love Mr. Lotte? All of us do, surely, even though his dull-penciled handwriting is impossible to read and he has tea-breath halitosis. But he lets us attempt songs far beyond our skill level just for the fun of it, like "Jingle Bell Rock" and the theme to *Fame*. He doesn't shame us when he assigns the same song for the third week in a row because we just can't get the hang of it. He doesn't charge too much for lessons, God love him, because he understands every father wants to give his daughter a chance to learn from the best.

Mr. Lotte likes to use the blinking metronome to keep the time, his female students have said. Or slap his knee. That's where it begins, at least. His hand roams to the steady progression of a well-played sonata. His knee, your knee, his thigh, your thigh, your back, your shorts, your top. A song in 4/4 time. ONE, two, three four, ONE, two three four. For him, the students wait in line.

To her parents, a young girl comes forward. "He put his hands on me," she says. "To the beat of the metronome." Then another comes forward, then another, then another. ONE, two, three, four. ONE, two, three, four. *TOCK tock tock tock.*

Over the years, he's taught close to a hundred students. Seven speak up; the rest of us remain silent. On the elementary school playground by the overturned basketball hoop, the spot where infatuation used to go to seed, boys and girls are now trying to snuff the snitches out.

Was it you? Was it you? Was it you? Was it you?

Word travels fast, and the culprits become known. Carly, with her sweet voice and her buckled shoes. Layne, with her piercing eyes and her basketball. Aria, with her fair skin and sheaves of drawing paper.

As Mr. Lotte goes, so goes the town. His first task was to separate us from each other, and Mercury follows suit. From this moment, all of Lotte's students stand on opposite sides of the yes-no boundary line, one side choosing what the other has not. For our silence, we'll remain safe and anonymous, the musical's *figurantes* who don't have any lines.

For their honesty, the other girls' reputations will be stained. They'll be called liars, even though they told the truth. All of us will think that girls just weren't meant to trust each other. There used to be an "us," the girls who once spent our afternoons at the park, our evenings reading books, and our phone conversations talking to each other. But that was before girls stopped being girls and started being targets. We had no choice but to scatter. Nineteen ninety-two marked the year of a great diaspora borne from a shared secret we've never spoken of. We have to believe there must be others like us who never said a word. There *must*.

Denouement

IT WAS EARLY EVENING by the time our last performance, a Sunday matinee, ended. The audience cleared out quickly, eager to return home before nightfall. In winter, we tended to stay in after dark. Hurry home, close the door, turn on the lights, stoke the fire.

After I packed away my scuffed shoes and damp tights, I began the process of unbecoming, unzipping the dress, letting down my hair. Now in jeans and a sweatshirt, I stood over the clothing donation bin and tossed my costumes inside. Julia stood at the opposite end of the emptied hall, motioning for me to hurry up. It was time to go; the cast party at the new house of the choir director, Mrs. Todd, had already begun.

We hopped inside my sister's friend Beth's car and shivered.

"It's gonna take a few minutes to warm up," she said, turning the defrost knob all the way up.

We stayed silent as we drove. The town lampposts whizzed by us, their glaring reflections slippery on the backseat. Nighttime in summer had felt like a deep well I could swim inside of, but this winter night kept its distance, a wide, black sheet not to be penetrated.

The road that led us toward Mrs. Todd's house wound through the frozen countryside to the farthest edges of town where a housing development had been built around a large manmade lake. It was a portrait of 1980s glamour—the cabins, clubhouses, boats, Jet Skis, and private docks—an ideal location to shoot a low-budget horror flick. Picture it: a group of unsuspecting teens spends a weekend in the woods, skiing, drinking, swimming, hoping for a relaxing getaway. It's all fun and games until a dead body washes ashore. A classic whodunit.

The clock is ticking for the remaining teenagers to figure out the killer's identity before it's too late.

On one of my first nights at the lake, I'd been invited to an eighth-grade boy's birthday party. A friend and I attended together, and her parents dropped us off. We stood in front of the house, the lake at our backs. Though we entered together, that was the last I saw of my friend until we left. She disappeared into some unseen back room with a boy. No matter how many of my friends started to test their limits, I wasn't the kind of girl who would go into a dark room with a boy I'd seen at a party. The reward wasn't worth the risk. Everyone would see, everyone would know, everyone would talk.

For most of the evening, I sat in a chair by the window. I didn't mind that no one seemed to notice me. The whole house was dark and packed with kids. The window gave a clear view of the lake in the distance; I watched it glimmer in the night, the lights from the surrounding houses shining across it. The place, not the company, arrested me for the first time, and it would many times after. Though I'd lived in Mercury all my life, I still found moments where I clasped the tragic beauty of this place around my neck like an heirloom necklace.

"There it is," my sister said, leaning forward in the passenger seat. "Turn left here."

We turned onto a gravel road and traveled up a low-grade hill. As we crested it, the glow from Mrs. Todd's new house cast shadows on the litter of cars already crowding her front lawn. About fifty yards away, woods abutted the property. The house beamed against the night. Even in the car, we could hear the dull noises of our cast mates laughing and shouting. The front door was open, revealing a thin glass door that allowed us to see into the foyer. The house exuded warmth, every hue cream and gold. We jumped out of the car and sped toward the door.

Inside, we stepped onto a landing halfway between the upper level and the basement. The house glimmered with ivory walls and gilded accents. Every floor teemed with teenagers, even the stairs. I followed

Julia to the basement where we found Mercury's typical party totems: baskets of chips cradled in greasy napkins. Mini-pretzels. A sheet cake with frosting thicker than the cake itself. A stack of red plastic cups. Hot wings from Coyote's Pizza.

A recording of the musical looped on the television, and I sat down against the wall to watch it. A couple of kids behind me goofed off with the "Chinamen's" hats from the play. The hats were so big that only their chins stuck out from beneath the brim. The two began to spar with plastic butter knives until one of them ran into the food table and knocked over the cups.

The sound on the video was spotty and much of the tape was fuzzy. Even so, a bunch of us sat and watched. Join us for our favorite pastime, become part of the spectacle: sit down and watch us watching ourselves.

I hadn't realized during the performance that Pete was chewing gum, but I could see his jaw bouncing up and down every time he came on stage. I watched the final bows, the leads point to the pit band and clap. A blurry finger appeared up close in the lens, hunting for the "off" button on the video camera. Then the screen flickered to neon blue for a few seconds before the beginning of the tape started to roll again.

I sat with my knees to my chest, eyes glazing over. The silhouettes of latecomers shuffled into empty seats. I felt sleepy. The other cast members chatted and goofed off around me. I had never minded being alone in a crowd, seeing the hazy shadow of my own profile cast against the wall from the light on the television screen.

I didn't notice when the chatting and teasing died down to murmurs. I didn't notice when the murmurs faded to whispers. But I did notice when five or six pairs of eyes gawked at me instead of the screen. I had that sick feeling of being watched, of my name slipping from someone else's lips. It was a sensation I'd learned to divine and sought to avoid. When I turned my head, the gawkers looked away.

I stood up. "What?" They ignored me. "What?"

I felt hot. I hadn't seen Pete since I arrived.

I crept toward the stairs. A clump of stifled giggles resounded from the second floor. On the stairwell, I passed the play's vicar, the steward, and the newspaperman who still wore his floppy fedora. Their blank expressions—still caked in stage makeup—looked maudlin and past their prime.

I spied the floor of the living room before I reached the top of the stairs. My head, level with the carpeted floor, appeared between two stakes of cast-iron railing that bordered the living room. About ten feet from me, a blanket had been suspended from the chimney, the corners splayed out on the ground into a makeshift tent. It was just large enough for two people to fit inside. A few of the Angels and sailors stood by. None of them saw me.

This was the best way to expose the truth in Mercury. Not what was told to you but overheard, not what was witnessed but spied. Two people lay entwined beneath the blanket. I recognized Pete's socks attached to the legs that sprouted out of the tent. They were white, cuffing just below the ankle. Those were the feet that were often propped on the coffee table in my parents' basement, the feet that tucked behind me when we watched scary movies and sipped from the same can of orange pop.

Every light in the living room had been switched on, and the space radiated. This charade had an audience. When Pete's head finally wound its way out of the tent, there was no mistaking it. He knew that I'd seen him, and seeing was everything in Mercury.

The following day during seventh-period chorus, we started to dismantle the musical set. When I arrived, some of the students were tearing out nails, unscrewing screws, and making a heap out of the wood that used to be the deck of the SS American just the day before. The crates where Pete and I kissed in the dark had been toppled and swept into the pile. Someone handed me a broom and I started to

sweep the stage. A few people asked if everything was all right between Pete and me. I told them it was.

Earlier that morning, I tried to hide myself in the shadow of my
locker door when I heard the laces of Pete's basketball shoes slapping
the ground as he hurried toward me. I stared at the picture of him in
his soccer uniform that I had taped to the inside of my locker. It made
me angry with him, angry with myself.

"I'm sorry," he said when he reached me. His voice cracked.

"Everyone saw you, Pete. Everyone."

"I'm sorry. I was just being stupid. That's all. Just stupid." He swal-
lowed and took a deep breath. "I am so, so sorry."

I looked at him and felt my anger melting to hurt. I hated that I'd
given him the ability to hurt me. I felt like that girl who couldn't catch
her breath so long ago, trapped beneath the inner tube in Carly's pool.
Pete's eyes were wide and the corners of his mouth turned down. His
face looked pale.

I'd promised myself at the beginning of last summer that he
wouldn't get any second chances. For Pete, I'd break one rule, but no
more. My reputation—my survival—depended on it. I blamed Virtue,
just as I was taught. Boys will be boys, and girls ought to know better.

"Let's just forget it," I said, retrieving my book. "Just forget it."

Later that afternoon, the auditorium air filled with dust and glitter
as we swept up the debris.

On the left-hand side of the backstage area, there was a gray cement wall. Some of the older kids who had leads in the play were
signing their names on it in permanent marker. They didn't sign their
formal names, but the names they were known by. Rudy. Chappy.
Wilp. Meatball. Some listed their characters' names as well. Moon-
face Martin. Evangeline Harcourt. Elisha J. Whitney. *Anything Goes*,
1996.

Pete and I signed our names side by side along the edge of the
wall. Permanent marker felt definitive. Lasting. We didn't know then

that the building would be renovated in a few years, and at that time, the whole wall would be demolished and all the names with it.

Despite my good intentions, my heart would not be roused. I was a girl Pete wanted only in the dark, and I couldn't remain there. If I lingered in the darkness too long, it threatened to snuff me out.

The evening of the cast party just confirmed what I already knew—there was no privacy in this town. If a girl gave a guy a blow job, everybody knew. If he unhooked her bra, everybody knew. If they pulled over on a dirt road to do it in the backseat, everybody knew. If he cheated, everybody knew.

After the school year ended, I told Pete I needed a break, and we both cried. It didn't matter how much I loved him. That need paled in comparison with my need to wash my hands clean of rumor, to pry my name out of the abyss of other people's mouths. My heart obeyed one commandment and served one master: I refused to be the girl everybody knew.

♪

As the fall of 1991 draws to a close and the weather grows cold, a chorus of voices gives sound to the wind. Whispers. Accusations. Denials. Could it be true? Could Howard Lotte really do such unspeakable things? The gossip travels to the grocery store, the post office, the library, the school. To football games and pep rallies and mailboxes.

This is a witch hunt!
    Just horrible rumors.
        Don't believe everything you hear.
And Mr. Lotte?
    People are treating him to lunch.
        You know, for support.
And so and so?
    Yeah, she's definitely one. And so and so?
        Yeah, she's another.

She's always seemed like a snitch.
 A tattle.
  A liar. It's definitely not true.
Maybe it's true.
 These girls and their imaginations.
  Blown out of proportion.
Is it worth ruining his life?
 He's a nice man.
  Everyone thinks so. Why all the fuss?

While those of us who are Lotte's most obedient students do our best to appear naïve, some of the townsfolk take it upon themselves to inform the judge assigned to Lotte's case about the true nature of the conflict at hand. Oh, we've got trouble right here in Mercury, they say. Trouble with a capital *T* and that rhymes with *G* and that stands for *GIRLS*.

In the months before Lotte takes his oath on the stand and the letters are made public, his supporters pen their treatises, their missives, their pointed accusations. One concerned couple writes in a letter to the judge that "as far as the charges which have been brought against Howard, we refuse to believe them. We find it a bit too coincidental that all of the accusers are associated with the Pure Heart Presbyterian church." Never mind that this statement is untrue. Many of the girls attend Pure Heart, but not all.

Someone else finds it "impossible to believe that a minor group of childish persons have been able to influence the judicial system to issue these charges." Another impassioned patriot claims Mr. Lotte is a "victim of perceived impropriety and parental hysteria." It goes on and on, the letters insisting the charges were "prefabricated by the students involved" and "a result of conspiracy." When all else fails, be assured that the people of Mercury know what's what.

Our town starts to get a reputation for falling apart at the seams, and for the first time, the cracks can't be blamed on the fall of the steel industry. On June 3, 1992, a local paper documents the results of the spinning rumor mill: "Since the investigation began last October, the town has been divided among those who are horrified by the thought of a teacher, who worked so closely with so many children, having this problem and those who believe Lotte was 'set up' by the young students who ranged in age from 9 to 13."

This phenomenon is what Lotte's lawyer will dub "an unfortunate turn" when he addresses the judge in late summer of 1992. He'll say that the case has "taken an unfortunate turn in that the children victims in this case somehow turned out to be the defendants in the eyes of many people." How unfortunate, indeed, as if a day of rain has spoiled our summer picnic.

Can you picture it? Half a dozen girls gather in an empty school yard after the day's final bell. In between the time slots scheduled for afternoon snacks and evening homework, the girls hatch a plan to take down one of Mercury's most untouchable men. Maybe one of them steps to the center of the circle. *I've got an idea*, perhaps she says as the other girls lean in. *An idea that will really get him good.* Before the sun sets, the girls—none of whom are trouble makers, all of whom get straight *A*'s—make a pact and corroborate their stories, while any conceivable motive remains absent. Everyone knows girls in Mercury don't need a reason to misbehave.

Though we've separated ourselves from these seven witnesses who are braver than we can stomach, one thing binds us together after the investigation ends and we grow from children into young women. Every encounter we have with an adoring boy—every kiss, every spare glance, every love note slipped from hand to pocket—becomes some kind of proxy by which the town devises to turn us into fools. Though perhaps we are foolish for falling so deep in love with this place and these boys that we can no longer distinguish the difference, we can't help ourselves from returning to them. Besides, it's not love we're known for anyway. We are known only by what others have done to us.

Around here, a girl can't escape her reputation.

Breaking and Entering

A WEEK AFTER I BROKE PETE'S HEART, Nora and I broke into an abandoned house. It was the Fourth of July, just days after I told the only boy who'd ever loved me that I wanted to be alone. The summer already felt too long, and I was looking for a way to celebrate my new independence, which didn't feel as liberating as I thought it would. As usual, Nora came to the rescue.

We went to see a movie. The closest theater was thirty minutes away in Juniper, the old steel town where I used to take ballet lessons. I hadn't been back to see Martine since before the musical auditions. I was just about to turn fifteen and I had started to abandon things I'd once desired without much understanding of my own actions. Out of my self-spun cocoon, I was emerging as a girl-moth whose flight pattern was determined by events she could no longer remember.

The road out of town was a wayward one, headed toward mills that had stood empty for years now. They'd worked their way into the rest of our sagging landscape, and people barely noticed them anymore. On our way out, we wound through rows of corn and crowds of trees. Rusty trailers and double-wides, warning signs for leaping deer and turns sharp as bent elbows. "Too many accidents on this road," my mother always said. Makeshift crosses and matted flowers dotted the roadside, marking the spots where cars had collided.

I shuddered as we passed a cluster of shabby memorials. These poster-board signs were eerie with their elegies scrawled in Magic Marker. From a distance, you could mistake them for yard sale advertisements.

The signs had a way of lasting too long, after rainwater muddled the ink and the white crosses faded to gray.

About five minutes outside of Juniper's city limits, Nora's mother yanked on her husband's sleeve.

"Ted," she said. "Pull into that driveway."

"What driveway?" he asked.

"That one," Nora's mother answered, jabbing her thumb against the window. "By the 'for sale' sign."

"I don't see any 'for sale' sign," he said.

"Just turn."

The minivan slowed. In the roadside ditch, a sickly "for sale" sign slouched among a thicket of weeds. Its stake was bowed, the black lettering weakened by the sun. The van crunched down a slender strip of gravel, and I pressed my face to the window to see what had provoked Mrs. Stark.

The house was set back, withdrawn from the highway. From the backseat I examined it, a house I'd passed innumerable times but never noticed. A colonial constructed from blanched, orange brick, two pairs of dowdy white shutters clung to the façade, and one tiny window popped out of the shingled roof.

Because there was nothing but cornfields in Mercury, I was used to long car rides spent passing time and houses. Rumors flew back and forth about them, and the more withdrawn the house, the more spectacular the stories. I'd heard of houses with indoor swimming pools, rooftop staircases, and even one with a carousel horse. I'd never considered going inside one before. No house around here could ever live up to the stories told about it.

Though it wasn't much different from the others on Route 44, this house had an attitude like a pretty teenage girl caught admiring herself in a mirror. The anticipation mounted; the farther we traveled down the drive, the deeper the house seemed to sit. Beside me, Nora sat up on her knees, her gaze trained on the orange brick. As we neared it, the house ballooned in size.

"It's *huge*," Nora whispered, her hazel eyes squinting at the sunlight streaming through the window.

"I've *heard* about this house," Mrs. Stark said, as if the place had a reputation of sleeping around.

"Do you think anyone's home?" I asked, but soon I knew the answer. Dandelions overran the patched, dry lawn. The rusty basketball hoop had lost its net. Torn plastic bags with dated circulars smothered the front stoop. No one had been here in a long time.

The van jerked to a stop, and we hopped out. My eyes darted back and forth along the perimeter of pine trees. Surely someone would come and tell us trespassers weren't welcome on such an expensive property, even if it was neglected. *It has to be expensive*, I thought. *Just look how far it is from the road.* The owner must have forked over some real cash to pay for such pretty seclusion. I watched the tree line. No one showed. The cars breezing down the highway buzzed like passing flies.

The five of us—Nora and I, her parents, and her younger sister Nell—stood in a clump, gawking at the giant house. Closer now, I could see the aged siding: chipped bricks, some missing. From where we stood, the parched yard sloped down to the right, framed by dense trees.

"Will you look at this place?" Mrs. Stark said, taking Nell's hand. "Let's take a peek at the backyard."

"I bet there are some nice-sized windows back there, too," Mr. Stark added, trailing behind.

After they disappeared, Nora and I grinned at each other. She jutted her chin toward one of the front windows, and we crept toward it. I had to hoist myself up just to get my eyes above the window sill. Nora was taller and bound to get a better view. A few spider webs glimmered in the dim light from the window. A sitting room, I thought. With hardwood floors. Colonials always had a formal sitting room in the front. Our hometown was ripe with dated structures that we called "Victorian," mostly because that was the name of the arts festival our town hosted every July: Victorian Days. I cupped my hands against the pane and peered inside, but I could see nothing.

"There's gotta be a better view over here," Nora said, heading for the next window.

As I passed the front stoop, the doorway grabbed my attention. The peeling entrance was sheathed with a flimsy plastic screen door. The closer I got to the house, the bolder I grew, and a burning desire to enter it overtook me. I'd never before attempted such an overt risk. Deep down, I thought, *boys will be boys, and girls will get caught.* And deeper still: *boys will trespass; girls are trespassed upon.*

I wrapped my fingers around the handle and pushed the rusty button with my thumb. The screen door screeched as it swung open. A passing breeze roused a soft jingle. Beneath the knob, a glittery set of keys dangled from the keyhole.

I heard the Starks' muffled voices coming from the back side of the house and smiled at the shivers tracing my spine. I glanced at Nora, whose face was pressed up against the window, her calves flexed as she tried to peer inside.

"Nora!" I hissed. "Look."

She rushed toward me, her eyes blooming when she saw the keys. "Dude," she said.

As I fingered the keys, I felt powerful. I'd never had a set of keys, not even to my own home. I grasped the knob. It felt cool in my palm, despite the heat. My wrist turned, and the bolt dislodged. The door grunted as I pushed, and it gave way, revealing a sliver of darkness. A gust of sour air poured out from the house, as if it had been holding its breath. I grabbed Nora's elbow and squeezed. The two of us pushed the door open the rest of the way and stepped inside.

My clearest memories of Nora exist underwater. From the time we were ten—the same summer as Mr. Lotte's hearings—our mothers dropped us off at Silver Pulley pool, and we'd spend entire afternoons in the deep end, fishing for quarters. I whispered what I thought were my worst secrets between dives. This is how I remember my best friend: submerged, hair like dark silk, her eyes shining bright in the turquoise water, tiny bubbles escaping from her nose.

Nora's beauty was the kind that drew attention, though she barely acknowledged anyone who showered her with it. She strutted around the pool in a bikini, and I hid behind a one-piece and a towel. Nora floated and flirted, never feeling the need to lay claim on someone like I did. With glasses and a petite frame, I tended to be overlooked. Until I got contacts and Pete came along, at least. But I was never jealous of Nora because I saw the two of us as a pair. I took pride in her beauty, and she admired my intelligence, one a perfect complement to the other.

Since I'd started to date Pete almost a year before, Nora and I hadn't spent much time together. After I'd told Pete I needed a break, things with Nora had returned to what they were before I fell in love and put him first, as small-town girls are known to do. A newly reunited pair, we returned to our daily phone calls and weekly sleepovers. I had missed my friend.

"We aren't trespassing, are we?" I asked Nora as we stood in the dark foyer of the house. Now within the house's walls, I grew timid.

"Trespassing?" Nora repeated, her voice echoing in the hollow space. "Nah. Nobody's lived here in a long time."

The humidity thickened the air in the house, and it was hard to breathe. Tufts of dust, disturbed by our entry, shimmered in the meager light. Room by room, we strode through the vacant house. We began in the sitting room, a bare, indiscriminate rectangle. Next, we conquered the kitchen, opening every drawer and cabinet as if they were our own. I tried to flip on the lights.

"The electricity's been cut off," Nora said, opening a tired refrigerator. She held her nose.

The back living room was an eyesore. Tangerine shag carpet covered the floor, and fake wood paneling flanked the walls. One large window brightened the space, drawing out the stains in the carpet.

Exhilaration began to pump through me again. I'd never been in an empty house before. I'd only stood inside the bare frame of my own house when it was built ten years earlier. "This is where your room will be," my father told me, pointing above our heads. "Right now, we're standing in the garage." I smiled, delighted at what would become of a lot once used as a campground, with old marshmallows and hot dogs buried in the grass.

But this house wasn't meant to be seen. Nail holes littered the flooring, mold had crept into the oak cabinets, and that horrible orange color permeated every room. Hungry for more, Nora trounced through the first floor and up the creaky steps. I followed close behind.

At the top of the narrow staircase, light broke in through the doorways on both sides of the hall. The space felt both bare and shy, as if the second floor kept all of the house's riddles. We explored the bedrooms, enchanted. Each possessed an architecture all its own. I'd never seen anything like it. In the final room, the walls came together in a hexagon, resembling the spire of a castle. I paused at the threshold because of what I found inside: a small twin bed with a metal frame and an old, lined mattress on top. It was the only piece of furniture left in the whole house.

I couldn't stop looking at the bed, but Nora pushed past me.

"I want this to be my room," she said, twirling around.

"Why? The other rooms are bigger."

"Because. Look."

She went toward the window, and we looked out at the treetops along the edge of the yard. For the first time, I felt what it might be like to look out *above* the town that held me in its thrall, rather than beneath it.

"You can see everything from up here," Nora said.

"Your parents would never buy this old place."

"You never know." Nora turned and looked at the bed. "You know what I heard?"

"What?"

"I heard somebody died in this house. A young girl."

"You did not."

"Did, too," she said. "I swear. I bet she died in that bed." She thrust her finger at the mattress. "That's why this house is on the market. The owners don't want to live here anymore. Problem is, nobody else wants to live here, either."

"Where'd you hear that?" I asked.

"I heard my mother with some of her friends. They were whispering about some old brick house on Route 44."

"This place creeps me out," I said, watching the bed as my eyes played tricks on me. I swore I could see the imprint of a small, dead body.

"That's why I want it," Nora answered.

I smiled. Nora and I were infatuated with ghost stories, and we'd just found one of our own. Pete used to laugh at how frightened I was when we'd watch scary movies together. For a moment, I wished he had come along so I could feel the reassuring heat of his palm against mine. But I banished the thought. I had been the one to find the key and step inside the house. My best friend and I had done this together. I didn't need Pete. I had Nora.

Though I would never have told Nora because I didn't realize it myself, the house resembled what had become of my own memory of Mr. Lotte—abandoned, slanted, and odd. She and I had both been his students once, and we never spoke of him, still. Instead, the two of us stood in the tiny bedroom, staring at the white walls, staring at the empty bed, staring at each other. While keeping still, something happened to us in that house. *Retiré*, Martine would have coined this move the house performed on us, often used when one is trying to balance on one leg. *Retiré*. Withdraw. Though we couldn't have been there for more than a few minutes, a pocket of time opened and we were reaching neither forward nor backward, but deeper into that moment, deeper into the house itself, as if we'd entered one of C. S. Lewis's magic wardrobes. In years to come, I'd pass this place countless times on my way out of town, and the house—always empty—stared back as if it withheld from me my own secrets.

After Independence Day, Nora enrolled in a lifeguard training course. She was already fifteen, and by next summer, she'd be old enough to lifeguard. She fit the mold well. Not only was she an excellent swimmer, but she was leggy and tan. I had considered taking the course many times. I loved to swim. But when I pictured myself trying to pluck someone from the bottom of the pool, I knew I'd panic. I couldn't be trusted.

But Nora never panicked, even when she was afraid. She knew how to take charge, take responsibility, and take what she wanted for herself. One afternoon, a couple of weeks after she began training, she called me.

"What's wrong?" I asked when I heard her cracking voice on the line.

"It's my pap," she said. "He collapsed on our driveway this morning."

"What?" I said. I knew her grandfather. He was spry and stylish with the blinding smile of a game-show host. "What happened?"

"I don't know what caused it. But I had to give him CPR until the ambulance came." She paused. Her voice was barely audible. "I just learned how to do it."

"Is he—I mean, he's all right, right?" I asked.

Nora struggled to push the words out. "The paramedic told me I saved his life."

I exhaled. "That—that's—amazing, Nora," I stammered.

I, in fearsome awe of her, kept my mouth shut as I coiled the phone cord around my finger.

"I never knew I could do something like that," she said. "Save someone."

I think Nora felt as if she no longer knew herself. She'd saved her grandfather's life, and when confronted with her own power, she couldn't recognize it. I would always be endeavoring to find mine inside myself and come up empty-handed.

I didn't see Nora for a few weeks after her grandfather's emergency because my family had planned a vacation to Hilton Head. It wasn't often that we went so long without communicating, but I didn't think about her while I enjoyed the beach with my family. Pete appeared in my thoughts, unbidden. But I had made my choice, and I resolved never to turn back.

When I returned, I got an unexpected phone call from a well-meaning friend.

"You'll never guess who Pete's with now," she said.

With trepidation, I proceeded.

"Who?" I asked.

"Nora."

"Nora?" I croaked.

"I thought you should know," she said.

A choking sensation gripped me, though my throat was empty. I hung up the phone and rushed to the bathroom, hiding in the dark nook by the hamper. I sat in a ball on the cool floor and started to bite my nails. Nora had swooped in, snatching what I had abandoned. Even though she called multiple times over the next few days, I never answered.

I'd felt this kind of knife-edge betrayal once before when Mr. Lotte's investigation had just begun. Though he maintained his innocence, he also claimed he had fallen ill and needed to cut back on his ever-expanding list of students. One night over dessert, my mother broke the bad news to me—I would no longer be one of Mr. Lotte's protégés. I was so stunned that I dropped my ice cream sandwich. My mother held me while I cried and told me that Mrs. Lotte was especially sad to see me go. "I just love Amy Jo," she told my mother. Mr. Lotte had no such sentiments to offer, or if he did, I can't recall them. I only remember the feeling of losing my breath. I can't even remember if I'd already lied on his behalf or not.

My young mind couldn't register the possibility that he might have dropped me because of what he'd done. My heart only had that bleeding-out feeling it gets when someone you love plays a dirty trick on you, as I had played—however unknowingly—against the girls who told the truth about Lotte, and as I thought Nora had played against me with Pete. In my anger I couldn't see that Nora had simply done what all of us girls had been trained to do: take the boys and leave the girls behind.

That summer I lost my friend but kept my fascination with old houses. The following year, one summer after the break-in, I volunteered as a house-tour guide during the annual Victorian Days arts festival. I liked to think of myself as an expert because my grandparents used to own one of the famous houses in town, just a few doors down from the courthouse. But under their ownership, the house had fallen into disrepair. Unable to maintain it, they sold the house to a rich college professor who gutted and remodeled it. My grandparents downsized from a striking Victorian in the center of town to a small, one-bedroom apartment a few miles away.

"My blue-and-white kitchen," my grandmother said as her grown sons boxed up her porcelain. "I'm losing my blue-and-white kitchen."

I still remember that house, especially the darkened hallway of the upstairs. The faulty switches were always on the fritz. In one room, my grandmother kept her 1950s vanity with the circular mirror. In a cabinet along the floor, she stowed a black bag of dress-up clothes for my sister and I to play with when we visited. Inside it, we found threadbare gloves, mismatched high-heeled shoes, a strapless black dress, and a satin, long-sleeved wedding dress with a torn veil much like the one Julia wore in the final scene of *Anything Goes*. We always fought over who got to wear the wedding gown. We relished the feeling of parading around the grand house while our relatives exclaimed, "Everyone look! Look at the young bride before she goes off to marry."

For the house tour, I'd been assigned to a property on the east end of town. The coordinator hurried me inside just before the crowds arrived, and I took my post on the second floor outside a tiny room with a slender bed and an old sewing machine. A chain crossed the doorway to keep visitors out. *Look, but don't touch.* While I was alone, I dipped one foot inside the room, just grazing the floor's black-and-white tile. I wasn't so brave anymore without Nora beside me.

People barged in with their cameras. They each looked at me with expectation. I ought to have a story to tell, but I didn't. Ignoring their disappointment, I remained quiet until a tourist asked me a question.

"So?" he asked. "What happened here?"

For a moment, I thought he meant Mercury, that he meant us, this place that people pass through on their way to someplace else. *Mercury?* I want to say. *Everyone knows nothing happens in Mercury.* But deep inside the abandoned house in my chest, I knew it wasn't true.

When I realized the tourist was asking about the room itself, my response fell from my lips like water. "Well," I said, taking a small step toward him and flashing a sly grin. "They say that once, a long time ago, a young girl died in this very room."

I still relied on Nora, an estranged friend who now clothed herself with what I'd cast off, even as I hated her for it. My story inspired a hushed awe and the tourists backed away, taking care not to disturb any of the mundane items they mistook for relics.

♪

Like most of the old houses in Mercury, Mr. Lotte's house is stuffed with mundane items that are often mislabeled as antiques. We've fingered the Christmas ornaments and old candy canes atop the Lotte's Christmas tree during the past holiday seasons, and we've spied the porcelain plates and state spoons from their viewing shelf above the staircase. Bits of Americana and craftsmanship have found their way into even the tidiest of Mercury homes, but all these items are just for show. The most functional item in Mr. Lotte's employ must be his electric metronome, which sounds off during every lesson, and during the fall of 1991, its ticking decreases by half. *Tock tock.* Once the investigation begins and the police start making their rounds, poor Mr. Lotte develops an odd case of sickness. Mono, some say. Stress, say others. Either way, he insists the illness has nothing to do with the investigation. He is innocent; all this is just bad luck. It's been a tough year all around. Still, his schedule is too frantic. He has too many piano appointments, too many commitments. He has no other choice but to drop some of his beloved students.

Those of us who will lie on Lotte's behalf can't identify those of us he kept and those of us he discarded because of the masquerade that has become our sleepy Rust Belt lives. Like insects preparing to cocoon, we prefer solitude over camaraderie. Even so, the same question teases each of us, and it isn't *why* he did it. We know that the strong will target the weak. We've felt it in science class before dissecting our dead frogs. But how do the strong choose their prey? We want to know *how* Mr. Lotte selected the girls on whom he let loose his addiction. He could have physically overpowered all of his students, so we figure he must have separated out those he'd conquered psychologically, the ones he deemed emotionally weak. Is that what he saw in us when he looked down from his perch on the piano bench? And of course we can't help but wonder if he used this same algorithm for which students to cut when his health took a turn. Did he first prefer the weak and then decide to rid himself of them?

In the years to come, some of us will set out to prove him wrong. We'll grow up to host the high school's morning news and join the speech and debate team. We'll commit to looking older men in the eye. Others of us will sit in the back of the class, earning our quiet straight *A*'s and doodling on the backs of spare exam sheets. The desolate survivor's path isn't wide enough for us to travel it together.

After the police come and go and each of us does our duty, we'll return to Dr. Shaffer's orthodontist office to get our braces removed. For some of us, it will be months later; for others, it will be years. Sitting in the waiting room for the last time, Pam-the-receptionist's repetitive jingle won't seem so funny anymore.

"Good morning, Dr. Shaffer's office, Pam speaking."
Drill buzz drill
"Good morning, Dr. Shaffer's office, Pam speaking."
Drill buzz drill

As the minutes pass, we don't bother to look through the old magazines lying in a heap on the corkboard coffee table. Instead, we just watch Pam and start to wonder if there's even anyone on the other end of the line. As if, when she wakes up in the morning and shampoos her hair, when she drives home after five o'clock, when she scrubs her family's dinner potatoes, she's always saying the same thing. Good morning, Dr. Shaffer's office, Pam speaking. As if she continues to tell herself *this must be true, this must be true, this must be true*, in order to get herself to believe it.

Throughout the fall and into the spring as the investigation proceeds, Mr. Lotte continues to teach his other students who made the cut. They are some of his best—the ones adept enough to tackle Pachelbel's "Canon in D" and the watered-down score to *Les Misérables*. Convinced of his innocence, the parents keep surrendering their five- and ten-dollar bills to him each week. The people of Mercury don't bail when the going gets rough. This we know for sure.

At school, kids in the hall prowl for details.

"Hey," they say to us. "You take lessons from Mr. Lotte, don't you?"

"*Used* to," we answer as we elbow our way through the crowd, headed for the solace of our desks. "Just leave me alone."

When we reach our desks, we exhale and pretend to study our books until class starts, and so do our recitations.

"Ain't ain't a word, people!" the teacher begins. We are learning that the mechanics of language are like the pistons in an engine of an American-made Ford. The verb pushes the noun. They pull and they push, pull and push.

"Repeat after me," the teacher commands. "I pull the wagon."

I pool the wagon.

"Not 'pool.' That pronunciation is incorrect. Try again. Pull."

Pool.

"No, pull."

Pooool.

We make fun of the teacher during recess in the school yard with our own recitations, anything that will keep our lips moving and keep them from telling the truth.

Repeat after us:

Don't say ain't, *your mother will faint. Your father will fall in a bucket of paint. Your sister will cry, your cat will die. The dog will call the FBI.*

We say it over and over and over, this Rust Belt recitation that keeps our mouths busy and compliant. This kind of doggerel occupies our minds until it becomes a feeble prayer to dumb us, numb us, become the sum of us—just like Pam and her receptionist's jingle, just like our teacher and her nursery rhyme, and just like the gossip running wild in the town of Mercury.

Torch

I WAS LONELY AFTER LOSING NORA, and my soiled heart needed the oddest kind of elixir. I sought solace with the best company Mercury had to offer—church boys. There was no better place to retreat than to the leftover scraps of a campground on Lake Erie, one so beloved by the youth in our town that we couldn't see how it barely staggered along. Each summer, I found myself most alive in a place that was almost dead.

On the first Sunday of Pure Heart Presbyterian's summer camp, the sun blistered as my friend Aaron and I sat on a weathered picnic bench in a clearing at the campsite. Aaron had been a constant companion through years of elementary school, middle school, Sunday school, and church camp. We'd gone through confirmation together just last year, now official members of the Presbyterian faith (or "Presbear-terian," as my brother Seth's favorite T-shirt coined it). Even then, Aaron hadn't worn a tie.

It was midafternoon, and the mood was quiet. The campers would be arriving in about a half hour, attached to fathers in gleaming pickup trucks and mothers with stamps for letters home. The parents would inspect the crooked mess hall, the gray beach, the rusting toilets, the soggy shower-room floor. They'd frown, and then they'd head for home, hoping for the best.

Now old enough to be counselors-in-training, or CITs, Aaron and I had been charged with handling registration. We sat with our backs hunched, elbows on our bare knees. Water lapped up the dirty, tired shore of Lake Erie about three hundred yards away. Though we'd only been outside for an hour, both our necks were starting to burn. His white legs seemed to soak up the sun, the light disappearing into his pale flesh dotted with fine blond hair.

In his right hand, he held a cheap, royal blue, convenience store lighter. He didn't smoke back then. A Swisher Sweet cigar every now and then, maybe. Aaron, in years to come, could be tracked by an evolution of lighters—from the cheap ones bought in packs, to heavier models spanning the colors of the rainbow, to sleek black, and then ending with the Zippo. Not once did I see him with a match.

Every so often, the flame from his lighter would flare. He'd hold it for ten seconds or so and then release. In the valley, we could see one of the teenagers brought over from the Czech Republic for the summer. He was shirtless, mowing the soccer field. We liked to joke that the manager of the campground kept his staff chained in the basement, because we only saw them when they were on the job. Other than the faint buzz of the mower, there was little movement around us. Just trees, the sporadic caw of a seabird, the occasional surf loud enough to reach our ears from beyond the cliff.

The lighter. Aaron's arm leaned into mine as he lit it.

"What are you doing with that thing?" I asked him.

"Stuff."

"Stuff?"

"You know. Lighting fires. What do you think it's for?"

I laughed, and so did he. Aaron had gentle ways of poking fun, punctuated with a two-toned laugh, a "ha-ha" that chimed high, then low. I felt myself start to relax. I never had to worry about impressing Aaron, because Aaron didn't care to be impressed. The other CIT boys around us absently tossed a ball back and forth. Thwap, thwap. Rush, rush, from the shore. Thwap.

These church boys were the safe boys. They thought of nothing beyond the present, beyond the ways they could pass the time on yet another long Sunday. The schedule was always the same: Sunday school, the service, a luncheon or meeting, then youth group. These guys were pros at finding fun in places it didn't exist.

I'd known them since I was six, these boys who hadn't changed much and had no interest in appearing to be other than what they were. They didn't care how they looked. Mussed hair, old shirts, track pants. But they always smelled fresh, like fabric softener. Uninterested in games aside from sports, these guys wouldn't be caught dead at the local pool. Under no circumstances would they make a girl cry. They knew it would horrify their mothers.

Like the pool rats, this group had its own unspoken code. Their definition of a douche: he who tries too hard.

New shoes were trying too hard. Long hair was trying too hard. Earrings. Cologne. Sandals were okay at the beach and nowhere else. They'd rather die than be seen at a county fair. But at church, every Sunday, you'd find them in the pews by the piano. On Sundays, they believed in clean clothes.

Safe boys. I draped myself in them. There was Aaron, of course. There was always Aaron. Hoyce, aspiring film director and goatee enthusiast. Teddy, the sensitive misanthrope. Isaac, the guy who said if the world fell apart, he'd go into the woods and start shooting things so he'd have something to eat. Mikey, blond-haired blue-eyed army boy. Reuben "I'll do anything for a dollar" Miller, Rube for short. Nick, the amateur comic. That summer, they were saving my life and they didn't even know it.

Sweat filled the hollow of my back. I arched and fanned out my shirt. Aaron didn't appear to be sweating at all. He stared at his lighter.

"So," he said.

"So."

"Pete?"

I bit my lip. "Over."

Out of the corner of my eye, I saw one of his eyebrows raise slightly. "Yeah?"

I paused. "He's with Nora now."

Aaron gave out his two-tone laugh.

"I'm glad that amuses you."

He laughed again, but I wasn't hurt. Someone like Aaron wouldn't bother to spend the energy to say "that guy's an asshole," because it would mean that he'd decided to give him the time of day, which he hadn't.

Aaron was Pete's antithesis. Not friendly. Not interested in high school—academically or socially. Extremely cynical about almost everything except for odd, whimsical things like kittens, Trivial Pursuit, and the song "Bad, Bad Leroy Brown" by Jim Croce. Aaron was only an optimist where music was concerned. Though he'd been told he'd never be able to carry a tune, he still practiced playing his guitar every day.

"You're upset," he said.

"Nah," I answered, pretending to squint in the sun, as if the glare was making my eyes water.

He cast me a look out of the corner of his eye. I flushed. He hadn't bought it. I shrugged.

"It hurts," I said.

He nodded. That's how it was with Aaron—always catching me lying, always catching me telling the truth.

In the shallow valley below us, a few cars started to collect by the tree line. We heard muffled car doors opening and shutting. Squeals of children. Trunks popping. The week was about to begin.

Aaron sighed, and he turned toward me. His brow was furrowed, and I thought for a moment that he was going to hug me. My body stiffened. Aaron and I weren't huggers. He wasn't one to feel compelled to alleviate my pain. It wasn't that he didn't care. He just understood that sometimes things hurt, and there was nothing to be done about it.

I could see him swallow. His Adam's apple leapt up and then landed. His hand clutched his lighter, the flame strong. His thumb released, and the flame went out. Then he took his cheap, plastic lighter and thrust it into the flesh of my upper arm.

The burn made no sound. I flinched.

"Hey!" I yelled. "That's hot!"

On my left arm, two tiny red tracks of inflamed skin began to swell.

"You just burned me," I said, rubbing my arm. "Did you really just try to *brand* me with that thing?" I shoved his shoulder. "What do you think I am? A cow?"

Aaron's mouth dropped open. He wanted to say something, but couldn't find the words. He'd surprised himself.

"Sorry," he finally said. "I have no idea why I just did that."

But I think maybe he did, even if he couldn't find the words to say it. Aaron understood that sometimes it felt good to get burned.

The first night at camp on the edge of Lake Erie, we set ourselves on fire. After the campers went to bed, I waited outside in the dark, peering through the screen door of the tepid women's bathroom in the middle of the grounds. The air inside was moist, stagnant. In the distance, a crowd of teenage kids joked and laughed at the campfire. Fluorescent light dripped through the screen like water through a sieve, drawing a grid on the cement. A leaflike insect resembling a butterfly clung to the center of the screen, cockeyed and still. Below it hung a sign that someone had Scotch-taped to the door.

"Hello. I am a luna moth. I am almost extinct. Please do not slam the door."

I creaked open the door, tiptoed inside, slipped the door shut. I crouched to inspect the moth. It looked beautiful and dead. The moth leaned its face toward the light. I heard the echo of boys' laughter.

"Torch it! Dare ya! Torch it!" one of them yelled from about a hundred yards away.

I stared at the luna moth, who gazed into the fluorescence. Other insects and moths spun around above me, buzzing as they rammed into the light bulb. The luna moth just seemed to watch the others, close enough to feel the warmth of the light, far enough to keep herself safe.

Down the road past the bathrooms and all of the cabins, two boys dangled a stick with a sock speared at the end of it over the campfire. I watched them jockey the sock back and forth between them.

"Torch it. Dare ya. Torch it," one of them said again.

"Nah," said the other. "You torch it." The sock dropped into fire and disintegrated. The boys snickered.

What they were doing was nothing new. Being young in a town full of matches guaranteed any summer evening would end with someone suggesting that we set something on fire. I pulled up the hood of my sweatshirt as the night chill swept inland from the black chaos of Lake Erie. I leaned against the fence that separated the edge of the cliff from the steep drop to the beach, the lake to my back. There was nothing to see out there anyway. It looked like nothing, Pennsylvania's rocky edges. The water remained a polluted lost cause, just gray with freezer-burn foam at the crests of its waves.

We were fifteen years old, and someone was always burning something. Leaves, trash, rubber, flesh. Every boy owned his own Zippo. He flicked it open, flicked it shut. Becker, who was seventeen, thrust his lighter out at arm's length and ignited the flame. His friend aimed a can of insect repellant at it and sprayed. It burst—a bluish-orange flame ballooned from the tiny lighter for just an instant. We laughed. Something about it was very funny. The rest of camp was dark and the flash was all we could see.

Next, Becker doused his whole hand in bug spray. I started to get nervous. He flipped open his Zippo and lit his hand on fire, waving it around. His hand beamed electric blue, like the end of a lit match.

"Knock it off, guys," I said. "You're gonna get hurt."

They ignored me. I stepped toward them, about to protest, but Becker clapped his hands together and the flame vanished.

"It doesn't hurt," he says. "See?"

He showed me his hands. His palms were white and soft. The backs of his hands had grown tan from hours spent mowing lawns for money. He wiggled his fingers. He'd caught fire but hadn't burned. It was magic.

The group of boys followed Becker's lead. They lit one hand. Then two hands. Then two hands and one foot. They waved their arms around like two burning baton ends, saying, "Woooo! Woooo! I'm on fiya!" Then they all smacked their hands against their thighs, stomped their feet. The flames went out.

The next morning, the luna moth wasn't on the bathroom screen door anymore, and neither was the sign. I searched the cement and found the little luna moth, burnt up like a leaf. I felt sick. Someone had torched it.

The girl who hung the notice sat in the bathroom next to the communal shower. She cried, clutching her paper sign, her tight curls bobbing. She sniffed. "Why on earth would anybody do this?"

But she knew why. We all echoed the sound of this evanescent Appalachian existence. As soon as that luna moth left its cocoon, the clock had started to tick. It was only a matter of time before fire would prove what all of us were worth.

Though I never thought about the lie itself, I still remembered the moment just before the police interviewed me about Mr. Lotte, the moment I started to spin my own cocoon. I had a dress rehearsal for an upcoming mime performance at a church a few towns over that specialized in theatrics. The act was set to a worship song, the choreography a blend of sign language and dance movements meant to evoke emotion from the crowd. The body speaks in ways the mouth cannot.

Before the dress rehearsal began, eight preteen, would-be starlets shoved themselves into a tiny yellow bathroom with two stalls, each of us jockeying for space in front of the single mirror above the sink. As fifth graders, Carly and I were two of the youngest. We all smeared our faces with gobs of sticky white goop. Once it dried, the paint constricted the skin on my face and it cracked at the corners of my mouth when I tried to open it.

Toni, our dramatic performance madam, strutted around us in that cramped bathroom. She commanded us to keep our mouths shut to hide our stained teeth. She commanded us to dance for the Lord, not ourselves. Never ourselves.

In the mirror, I saw a white face, darkened eyes, black lips. The glass shone like a vanity in a Hollywood dressing room. A yellow ridge of rust circled the drain of a dirty sink.

"Watch me, girls," the madam commanded us. "Do as I do." Toni lifted her hands in the air and stretched. We did the same.

One by one, we raised our hands in the air, flames of white spreading from black sleeves. A still frame: I stared into the mirror with a blur of girls around me, our faces a legion of gaunt expressions, slick with white paint. My lips barely parted. My eyes darkening. My self disappearing.

On the ride home, my mother told me two policemen would be waiting at our house to ask me some questions. "You don't need to be afraid," she told me, placing a hand on my shoulder. "Just tell the truth."

But I'd already entered my hibernation. I'd made my choice.

Later in the evening at the Lake Erie campground, the boys formed a line and soaked their hands in bug spray. The sky darkened. Then I smelled the acid of insect repellant, I saw the gleam of a Zippo. The flame ignited one pair of hands, and those hands lit the next, and the next, and the next. The sky slowly lightened like the dark sanctuary on Christmas Eve during the annual rendition of "Silent Night," which

I'd always loved. Christmas was the closest I came to touching fire—once a year, I let hot Christmas Eve candle wax lose its form and drip onto my hand. I'd watch it harden and latch itself to my finger. I'd peel it off and leave the shavings on the floor. Every other night, even those heart-out-of-your-chest nights like this one, I kept a safe distance.

The last pair of hands in the chain went ablaze. They laughed at themselves for a minute, at how well they had cheated fire. Our way of life, our very selves, endangered but not yet extinct. Not yet. One by one, the flames disappeared. But the last boy hoisted his hands above his head and ran away from us down the stretch of camp past the bathrooms and the cabins, hands burning like two lit torches.

"On fiiiiiiiiiire!" He laughed as he ran.

The shallow waves of Lake Erie lapped against the shore at the bottom of the cliff, making the shards of empty beer bottles tinkle like the toast from a thousand champagne glasses.

"On fiiiire!" he screamed again as he looped back and sprinted toward the cliff. He ran straight toward the magnetic orange-blue campfire, like a moth to a flame.

♪

The winter of 1992 groans into spring as Mr. Lotte's investigation finally comes to an end and mothers everywhere breathe a collective sigh. After months of shushing their children's questions and swapping rumors with each other during the commercial breaks of their afternoon soaps, things will finally return to normal. Won't they?

See, there's an odd stench in the May air, and it puts us all on edge. Some people are beginning to suspect that Mr. Lotte *did* actually do it, and things in Mercury are starting to stink. Our fifth-grade social studies teacher, Mrs. Voos, does what she can to keep us on track, especially since it's the end of the year and all we can think about are Popsicles and pool parties. She has a much easier task than the sixth-grade teachers, who are all worried about their fellow educator and friend Mr. Lotte. The students are worried, too, and to show their devotion, Mr. Lotte is named their favorite teacher in the latest issue of our school newspaper. Someone also started a collection for his legal fees, asking schoolteachers to donate a hundred dollars each. Rumor stated that one of them even gave a thousand to the cause.

It's hard for us all to stay focused, but every day, Mrs. Voos stands in front of the chalkboard, her black orthopedic shoes spread wide. The early signs of Parkinson's disease cause the fingers of her right hand to rattle against the slate. Her penmanship has been in steady decline since the fall, and her sentences written on the board tend to look like they're going down a flight of stairs. It's hot out; a fan slowly turns at the side of the room. The sleeves of Mrs. Voos's floral muumuu flutter. She's teaching us to memorize all of the states in alphabetical order. In music class, we're learning a song about the presidents.

Martin Van Buren, William Henry Harrison, John Tyler, James K. Polk, and Zachary Taylor

She makes us color portraits of each of the forty-one American presidents, which we think is stupid. A string of men with white faces and white hair. What's to color? There is no peach-colored pencil, so all of their faces look either jaundiced or burnt. It's a waste of perfectly good drawing paper, and Mrs. Voos gives out more *B*'s than *A*'s.

Herbert Hoover, Franklin D. Roosevelt, Harry Truman, Dwight Eisenhower, John F. Kennedy

She tells us over and over about the day President Kennedy died, as if it's a movie reel soldered into the backs of her eyelids. "We all went home," she warbles. "Everything closed. And we all just cried and cried and cried. He was the best president this country has ever had. He was so handsome."

Mrs. Voos tells us she doesn't believe the rumors that he cheated on Jackie Kennedy. Everyone knows rumors are started by jealous girls. She also feels it's quite important that we know that Kennedy's secretary's name was Lincoln, and Lincoln's secretary's name was Kennedy. "A conspiracy!" she calls it. And don't forget that Lincoln was shot in Ford's Theatre, and Kennedy was shot while riding in a

Lincoln, which is made by Ford. Conspiracy! That word has become quite popular in Mercury these days.

We also learn all of the states and their capitals in alphabetical order.

Alabama Alaska Arizona Arkansas California Colorado Connecticut Delaware Florida

Sometimes when we are supposed to be learning about Tallahassee and Ponce de Leon, Mrs. Voos tells us about her husband instead. "He's waiting for me in Florida," she likes to say. "He's waiting. He's waiting and he can't wait for me to join him. He can't wait."

One day near the end of May, Principal Mellon's gravel voice comes on the PA system. "Attention. Attention everyone." He stops abruptly to tend to his smoker's cough. "There's been an explosion at the car dillership dahn the road. We're gonna evacuate the school. We're all gonna walk dahn to the high school."

In Mrs. Voos's class, Lorenzo Burk begins to cry. His father works in the auto shop at the dealership. "Quit it," Mrs. Voos says. "It's time to walk."

We walk through town, making a snaking line of lunch boxes, math workbooks, and dirty shoelaces to the high school where the buses are waiting to take us all home. Mrs. Voos drives her car to the high school, a mossy green Lincoln, made by Ford. Lorenzo cries almost the whole way. It's a beautiful day. The air smells like plastic.

In the parking lot, Lorenzo's mother is there waiting for him. He finds out his father survived the propane explosion. No one was hurt, even though the whole building was destroyed.

"See?" Mrs. Voos says. "I told you." She hobbles away toward her Lincoln.

"My husband doesn't like me driving everywhere by myself," she likes to say. "He doesn't like it."

We all think Mrs. Voos's husband has left her, but none of us wants to be the one to break it to her because it's the illusion that seems to keep her going. There are only a few days of school left before summer vacation, and no one sees Mrs. Voos again after that. We hear that she's fallen ill and is staying at home. We picture her sitting on a sofa with a ratty afghan across her ample lap, looking out her window toward the street, perhaps pondering the coincidence that both Lincoln and Kennedy were succeeded by men named Johnson.

While the air is still full of soot, Howard Lotte delivers a plot twist that makes the entire town gasp. We hear about it in school in the liminal space between the explosion and summer break. In May, Lotte hosts his final year-end recital near the center of town at Holy Ebenezer Chapel, a tiny white-and-black church with a red door. Soon, the formal court proceedings are scheduled to begin and everyone assumes Mr. Lotte is ready for a fight.

Right before the recital's reception, he dismisses the children to the basement for cake and punch while he addresses the parents, who—all still staunch supporters—have kept their daughters enrolled in piano lessons, testimonies be damned. He stands at the front of the chapel and looks out at the clots of parents seated throughout the pews. He tells them what a difficult year it's been (health problems and all) and that he's decided to give up the fight and plead guilty to the charges. So the girls won't have to go through the trial, he says. They've been through enough.

Mr. Lotte, not yet fifty years old, has resigned himself to Rust Belt martyrdom, but not if his supporters have anything to say about it. Before his sentence hearing on August 28, 1992, the judge receives more letters on Lotte's behalf. One writer takes the liberty to speak for many by stating that "it is our strong personal opinion that the only reason Howard pled guilty was his concern for the financial future of his family." Someone else points out Mr. Lotte's act of throwing himself on his own sword "speaks to his concern for the students." Mouths across town are lifting up the Lottes in prayer, as another concerned citizen shares with the judge, "My prayer is that his guilty plea is not the result of poor attorney advice."

One thing is clear—the town has had it up to here with this whole thing. Even if Lotte did touch the girls, is that really so bad? Is it worth all the dissention? We're a *community*, for Christ's sake. What will parents tell their children who have been assured of Lotte's innocence? As the news spreads from one stop sign to the next about Mr. Lotte's guilty plea, weary housewives sigh and look at their husbands as if to say, "Oh, now I have *this* mess to clean up, too?"

The impossible part is admitting that Lotte *might* be guilty, that he *might* have fooled us all, that everyone *might* have been wrong about him from the very start, and no one will even entertain the thought. Just like Mrs. Voos who keeps the candle of her heart lit for a husband who isn't returning, the people of Mercury know how to go down with a sinking ship.

PART II

Simon Says

Sober

JUST AS IT HAD IN 1973 when my father played for Mercury High School's starting lineup, football season rolled around again. At the first away game of the year, the September air steamed like the inside of a hot mouth. The stadium lights of the home team's field glared in the late daylight. There was nothing special about the day—a typical away game in a typical football season of a typical small town. We'd all done this before. But the perennial choreography in Mercury I'd learned to rely on now felt foreign for one reason: it was all the same, and I was not.

Relegated to the far side of the field, the "away team" bleachers stood at a distance from the bathrooms and concession stand. A chain-link fence guarded entry to the woods behind the stands. There wasn't a bird in the sky. The band moved as a unit, and—as we did at every game—once we entered the bleachers, we performed a corporate sit-down. The rotting stands bowed beneath the heft of the Mighty Mercury Mustang Marching Machine.

At halftime, we struggled through our performance. We hadn't worked out all the kinks for the new season yet. The peppy music I remembered from last year had melted into noise: the blare of the trombones and trumpets, the wailing of the piccolo, mixed with the fanatical screams of mothers who hoped to God their sons would see a good amount of playing time this season. The instruments played on, relentless, in a shouting match for prowess with the home team's marching band seated on the opposite side of the field.

They called: We've got SPIRIT, yes we DO!

We answered: We've got SPIRIT, how 'bout YOU?

Everything unfolded as it had the year before, a rendition of the same rites Trent Reznor used to perform when he was in the marching band fifteen years before. We wore the same outfits, performed the same dances. Pete sat in the same section of the stands, in the same Levis and backwards hat. But this time, I stared at him while he stared at Nora as she pranced around on the track with the other cheerleaders, her legs two tan stems, her black hair flopping as she bounced.

Since the end of July, I'd chosen to spend most of my time alone. When my sister left for college in August, the bedroom we had always shared felt empty. I felt myself falling prey to the kiss of death in our town—wishing that time would move backward, believing the past had the power to eclipse the present.

The week before school started, Pete and I collided on the practice field not far from where we once played Spotlight. The soccer team had scheduled practice on the field after marching band rehearsal, and I saw him from my position on the thirty-yard line, his body limned with the dark tan of his skin and the red of his practice uniform. He clenched a soccer ball to the ground with his cleat. Only a strip of skin gleamed from the hem of his shorts to the top of his socks. He stood at the top of the hill that sloped down to the level practice field, as if presiding over it. I'd imagined what this would be like, what we'd say.

The sting of solitude led me to rediscover my own nature—I worked best on my own. I gathered my secrets around me and clutched them tight, determined to look cold while my insides roiled in a white heat. It was the only way to keep myself from incinerating. In our demise, Pete had become a proxy for the town I loved but didn't dare trust, a town that I thought would split me open if given the chance. All of Mercury was waiting for me to bottom out, and for once, I refused to give the performance it demanded.

That day on the football field, Pete and I said nothing. My practice ended and we passed each other as I came off the field and he went on. He kicked his ball. I let my pom-poms dangle. I looked at the ground, he looked at the horizon. We didn't walk toward each other, our heads didn't turn, we didn't pause. Pretending to be strangers, we went our separate ways.

Later, I'd imagine that instead of passing each other, he'd come up to me, saying, "Hey," and I'd say "hey" back, and those three letters would reveal everything lost inside of me, lift the burden I buckled beneath, and Pete would pull me out of my own narrow pit. But my illusions began to dissipate as I realized one thing I knew to be true. If I wanted out of this place, I'd have to get out by myself. No one else could do it for me.

After the football game ended, I climbed onto the dark school bus and pushed toward my seat in the back. My bag, stuffed with my pom-poms, thumped against the seats as I passed.

"Watch it," said people with instrument cases and batons and plumed hats. The musicians were shedding their thick wool jackets, crafted to withstand the cold Pennsylvania weather in November. Cheeks were flushed, brows wet, and the air smelled of stale sweat and the spit that dribbled from the bell of a brass instrument. I suppressed the urge to gag.

I dreaded these chaotic rides. I slouched in my seat as someone in the front started a chant:

We are the Mustangs! The mighty mighty Mustangs!

I didn't join in, and no one noticed. I pulled my faded, careworn Levis from my duffle bag and slipped them on over my tights. The denim felt cool for just a moment before molding to my skin.

In the seat ahead of me, a kid who went by the name "Tip" turned around and tried to goad me into a staring contest. An army of pimples trooped along the line of his hat's chin strap, which he still wore, the plume standing at attention. I wasn't in the mood to play. He patted my forehead with his sweaty palm and then giggled before plopping into his seat.

I fingered the knees of my jeans where the denim had become threadbare from crawling on the ground during games of Spotlight. I couldn't see it in the dark, but I knew there was a grass stain on my left knee. I was glad when the blemish didn't disappear in the wash.

A series of bus windows snapped open, and kids let out their best wolf howls into the heavy night. I covered my ears with my hands and leaned against the window. I envied my band mates' lack of inhibition. Howling was something I'd only do somewhere deep in the woods with friends who knew me, friends like Aaron who would never come to a football game. Even as an avid baseball fan, he wouldn't be swayed to play for the local team. "You love the sport," I said once. "Why not play?"

"No ride to practice," he answered and shrugged. "Besides, what would be the point?"

Perhaps Aaron was right, and there was no point. That fall was a sobering one for me. I'd let first love in a small town hypnotize me, and when Mercury snapped its fingers, I'd awoken alone in the dark. As we rode home amidst an onslaught of whooping and catcalling aimed at no one in particular, I couldn't help but wonder where I'd left myself. This was the ruthless crash of getting clean.

A few weeks after school started, Pete and I crossed paths again. As he loitered just outside the cafeteria, we met by accident in a rare moment when no one else was around. I had been walking the hall with my head down, and when I looked up, he caught me in his sights. Headed straight for him, I couldn't look away. I couldn't pretend he was a stranger.

"Hey," he said.

"Hey," I answered. I kept my voice dead, but those words, those *words*.

He asked how I was. I claimed to be fine. Then I made a huge mistake.

"If you hadn't gone after my best friend," I said, "I would have gotten back together with you."

I didn't know why I said it. I hadn't intended to; it just fell out of my mouth. Stupid, stupid girl. Didn't I know honesty was never an ally? This was a truth I understood deeper than my ability to explain it. Pete stared at me, his face quizzical, as if trying to pinpoint at what moment I'd lost my mind. Honesty and desperation were bad enough, but both meant certain suicide. This wasn't the girl he knew. I was smarter than that.

Pete sighed. I felt my face redden. What had happened to me? I still kept a picture of the two of us from New Year's Eve in safekeeping, next to my fifty-dollar bill. The photograph was dark; we sat in lawn chairs in Sidney's unfinished basement. That evening he wore the green sweater I'd given him for Christmas. I kept telling myself to throw the picture out.

Five years after Mr. Lotte's investigation, no one ever talked about what happened except for a few brief moments when girls who'd come out against him had struggled in some public way—an eating disorder, a bad breakup with a star on the football team, an unfortunate choice to get drunk before a Friday night basketball game. These girls knew to blame themselves instead of Mr. Lotte, lest they be judged for turning him into a bucket of blame they could dump all their problems into. But when I look back at moments with Pete, with Nora, when I might have salvaged something important to me, Mr. Lotte is the only person I can see.

"I should go," I said to Pete, turning my head. I fled down the staircase, in search of some dark place to hide.

Something I wish I could forget: Pete and I in wintertime, lying on the couch in my parents' basement. Watching yet another unmemorable movie on yet another frigid night. A greasy bag of Hot Fries lay limp on the worn wooden chest we used as a coffee table. The tiny dusk-colored houses on the wallpaper of my parents' basement walls resembled faded polka dots in the half-light from the television screen. What I can't forget is how ordinary the evening was, how similar to every other Saturday.

Pete leaned his chest against my back, and my shoulder blades sank into his soft and sturdy skin. His hands found their way around my waist. His fingers were hot. They paused at the rise of my rib cage.

He leaned his lips close to my ear, and I felt his breath, the way his nose slid into the bend of my neck. I couldn't see his face.

"Do you want me to?" he said.

I tripped over his words in my mind. For reasons I didn't understand, I felt like crying. I couldn't think of my response, only his question. Only his thinking to ask it.

I shrugged.

He waited for just a moment and then hugged me. He must have felt how tense my body became. How rigid. We watched the rest of the movie in silence. His hands remained around my waist, at peace. His body, fluid. Mine, petrified. He left on time, even though my parents were asleep.

I thought of it even more after we were no longer together, this remnant of falling in love inside a corpse.

Though we couldn't escape each other, Nora and I had yet to speak. I had become an expert at ducking in and out of class and avoiding the hallway. I didn't want to see Nora and Pete together. When he visited her locker a few doors down from mine, I made sure I was already on my way to class. I repeated Martine's mantra, "Don't let them see you sweat," any time I thought Pete or Nora might be near. I felt love and hate for them both in equal measure, and my swollen anger defied all my attempts to quell it.

Near the end of September, I received a note from the school nurse during history class, directing me to visit her office. I had no idea why Mrs. March would summon me. I tried to steer clear of her—she had the look of impending death: a skull-like face, spindly fingers, drooping jowls with skin barely clinging to bone. Somehow, she'd gotten the nickname "Yutes" among the students, making every bizarre encounter with her even more awkward as I tried not to call her "Yutes" to her face.

When I reached her office near the junior high wing, I found Yutes just as expected, sitting in her black chair behind her black desk, engrossed in some report fastened to her clipboard. The tight office smelled like tongue depressors. I waited.

Slowly tilting her head toward me, Yutes gestured the knob of her pointer finger toward a closed door. "In there," she said.

I paused, hoping for further instruction, but received none. I stepped inside the room. There I found Nora, blotchy-faced and red-eyed, sitting on top of a padded examination table, a sheet of sanitary paper crumpling beneath her. I fiddled for a moment, unsure where to sit in a room that appeared to be a converted closet. Nora scooted over, and I hopped up beside her. Together, we stared at the wall.

"Are you all right?" I asked.

"I miss you," she said. "You and I used to do everything together."

Taken by surprise, I didn't respond. I had assumed Nora had been motivated to reconcile out of guilt. I'd never considered the possibility of her missing me even though I missed her. Boys were supposed to be a girl's cure-all; I didn't know one girl could break another's heart so fiercely, so swiftly. She had the ability to hurt me in a way Pete never could because I'd loved her in a way I hadn't loved him.

She continued. "You've put up this wall. I can't get through to you."

My sense of betrayal kept me stone-faced. "This is about Pete," I said.

"This is about you and me."

"I don't know what you want," I said.

Nora didn't answer. Outside the door, Yutes tottered in her chair. Normally, I would have made a joke at Yutes's expense, and Nora would have told me to be nice. She was always thinking the best of people, and I was always telling her people can't be trusted. This was why we were friends—we made each other better. I still thought of Pete as my property, though I had vacated it. Nora had become the squatter, but she was partly right. This wasn't about Pete or who belonged to whom. Nora and I were both opportunists; we both wanted out of this town, we both wanted to be more than just some girl from Mercury. The same quality that had first attracted us to each other now repelled us. But here she was, reaching a hand toward me, and I wouldn't take it. This was the ghostly toll of a lie I'd told long ago—numbness was replacing the space inside me where emotion once had lived.

"Well," I finally said.

"Well," she said.

I didn't ask her if she and Pete were really together. I knew she hated that kind of question. I didn't ask her to apologize, either. I knew she wouldn't.

After more silence, she slid from the bed and walked out, leaving me alone.

On my way back to class, I took my time through the empty halls. Nora's words echoed: "You've put up a wall, a wall, a wall." She still knew me better than anyone else.

My own capacity for coldness startled me. My friend had sobbed while I sat next to her, and I didn't even flinch. The truth: I feared how deeply I could love someone, and not a boy, though a boy was the crown of every young beauty in Mercury. The love to be feared most was the kind one girl had for another. That kind of love had the power to unearth deep secrets, to dismantle the selves I'd constructed, to make me whole in a way I feared would cost me everything.

As it had with Nora, this fear often manifested itself as jealousy. Just before the rumors about Mr. Lotte began to swirl and the townspeople would identify my friend Carly as a troublemaker, we sat in class with a few other friends at the beginning of our fifth-grade school year. When Carly stood up from her desk and turned her back, I pointed out to the other girls how her black stretch pants sagged around her butt. "Carly pooped her pants!" I said, because I envied how perfect and beautiful and beloved she always was. We laughed, and she turned around and started laughing too, not wanting to be excluded.

"What are you laughing at, Carly?" I asked. "We're laughing at *you*."

She looked stricken, and I felt immediate regret. Soon she would forgive me without an apology. What troubles me most is that I can't throw this memory into my own receptacle of blame for Howard Lotte. My insides were crooked long before the lie ever left my mouth.

♪

Carly's father, Charlie Knox, has one of the most glamorous jobs in town—he's the manager of Rip's Sunrise Market, Mercury's only grocery store (until Giant Eagle opens across from the courthouse, that is). But Giant Eagle doesn't stand a chance, what with Rip's Sunrise Market's reputation for baggers who will push your cart through the crowded lot and load your trunk with groceries. The baggers won't even accept tips because it's ungentlemanly, and what would we do if one of them saw us shopping at Giant Eagle? It would be nothing less than a personal affront, and the mothers across town will have no part in it. Besides, the word on the street is that you have to bag your *own* at Giant Eagle. What does Mercury need with two grocery stores, anyway? One suits us all just fine, and that store is run by Charlie Knox. We young, naïve girls think managing a grocery store must mean the Knox family has money because managing is synonymous with owning, isn't it? Never mind that the store is named for some unseen "Rip" character. There are a lot of things we don't yet understand.

During the day, Mr. Knox can be found within the confines of his meat-and-produce domain, emerging through the thick plastic strips that separate the store from the back warehouse or pushing a tall, rolling tray of bread next to the deli meats. His daughter Carly is following in her father's footsteps, selling hard root-beer candy for a penny out of the open window of her playhouse in her parents' yard when she isn't practicing piano or her ballet routines. But after Howard Lotte's investigation begins, the Knox family can't continue life in Mercury as they had before.

When Carly's father takes the stand on August 28, 1992, during Mr. Lotte's sentence hearing, none of us are present to hear him speak. The courtroom is no place for children. We're probably back-to-school shopping at Kids-R-Us or painting our nails or writing in our diaries while taking the extra time to draw hearts over the *i*'s, trying hard to forget anything that happened with Mr. Lotte. We're wiling away the hours before we return to the school where he will no longer be a sixth-grade teacher. His room will be occupied by an unfortunate replacement who must work within the memory of a living martyr, a room that will remind everyone on both sides of the Lotte "incident" what is wrong with our town.

Although Lotte has pled guilty, rumors of his innocence are still quite robust in Mercury, so the judge has asked for spokespeople from both sides to testify at the hearing. Five parents of the victims will take the stand, and seven will speak on Mr. Lotte's behalf, including Lotte himself. Most of those speaking on Lotte's behalf are fellow teachers, many of whom teach the grade Carly will be entering in September. When the judge asks her father to share how the "incident" has affected his family, he does his best to put the feeling into words:

> You can't explain what it's like to have a daughter come home and cry and say: Dad, this stuff happened to me; and the school's raising money to protect this man. Don't they believe me? Do they think I'm a liar?
>
> And when you think it's all over and you say: Well, finally the man will plead guilty and it will all be done. And it's not over yet. We still walk around town like we are the criminals, and we are nothing but the victims.

Even someone like Carly's father knows that we—the unspoken, the liars—exist, though we persist in hoping that our diaspora will suggest otherwise. He states that "there's many, many that haven't come forward because they weren't willing to take the ridicule." And here we thought we'd outwitted an entire town with our faux naiveté! Did our own parents ever wonder if we had lied to save ourselves, or was it just as easy to believe in Lotte's stronghold of virtues along with everyone else? Did you know he plays the organ for the Sunday morning choir, for goodness sake? We've cast our lot with him, no pun intended, and there's nothing we can do now. Somehow, we're liars either way—if we say he didn't touch us, and if we say he did. Nothing will soil a young girl's splendor like being called a liar or a potty mouth. To lie is bad enough, but to lie about *this*? There may be no hope for saving us.

When reading Carly's father's testimony, it's difficult to discern who the true perpetrator is: the man who enacted the crime or the town that protected him. Can you feel it, the bitter chill of an entire town turning its back? Mr. Knox's final words are of his daughter, and they include a prescient hint toward their future:

> This past week, my daughter came to me in tears and she said: Dad, don't send me back to that school. Don't send me back to that school. And so I've had to take her out and put her in a private school; and we walk around town, and people look at us like we did something wrong. This is America. Why should we have to pay the price?

The cost of truth is hefty, indeed. Soon, Mr. Knox will no longer be found in the aisles of Rip's Sunrise Market. We won't get a chance to say goodbye before Carly starts attending private school. Soon the whole family will leave their swimming pool and Carly's playhouse behind when they move to a neighboring town. Within a few years, they'll move out West to start over, and who can blame them? Mercury is not a place anyone comes to begin again.

Vanity Fair

IF I WANTED TO SAVE MYSELF from becoming just another girl in Mercury, I was in need of a man whose actions I could mirror. I found him on opening night of the annual school musical, just after I'd gotten a bloody nose. Throughout its short run in the auditorium, *Li'l Abner* and its flat notes were rewarded with tepid applause. Even so, the Mercury High School auditorium was packed for the first show. The pulleys creaked as the curtain opened on just another day in Dogpatch, a town hidden in the Appalachian hills. The set was bare, just an art-room mural of some smoky mountain in the background and the façade of a broke-down cabin.

The cast didn't need to shop for costumes at the Salvation Army that year—we all had the wardrobe for the part. Flannel. Old jeans, cut off above the knee and dark eye shadow smudged across our cheeks. Our inspiration for the characters we portrayed relied on the pillar of hillbilly self-esteem:

There is always someone more redneck than you.

The bloody nose came when the Dogpatchers realized we'd been voted the most unnecessary town in the country, and we broke out in a square dance. The Dogpatchers paired up, boys with girls, to hoedown. Heel-toe, heel-toe. Swing that partner round and round. Pick her up and put her down. During rehearsals, this number had caused all of the female chorus girls gross amounts of anxiety because the choreography called for the boys to hoist us in the air. Were they strong enough? Were we too heavy? Some of the girls in Mercury could eat and drink the boys under the table—though neither the boys nor the girls wanted to admit it.

The climax hit when the boys threw the girls over their shoulders and trotted around in a circle. Mercifully, no one fell. The song concluded and the audience applauded. The boys swung us down. But the boy beside me was too close and the wooden high heel of his partner's shoe cracked me in the nose on her way to the floor. I didn't even see it coming. I'd never seen stars before, but I saw them that night, shining against the black auditorium. I blinked a few times and held my pose. *Never let the audience see your mistakes*, Martine always said. *I don't care if your costume comes off.* My head teetered as I struggled to hear whether or not the applause had ended. I realized everyone else was running offstage and the transition music had begun. I followed the rest of the cast into the dark wings.

"So sorry!" the girl beside me whispered. "Are you okay?"

"It's nothing," I answered as my eyes started to tear. She apologized again before running off for her costume change. My head dizzied. I sniffed and slid the ridge of my finger beneath my nose. A line of red ran the length of it.

Once my vision righted itself and the bleeding stopped, I rushed into the choral room to change into my next costume, a barely there skirt with a gold sequin belt and a matching army-green top and a military cap. Along with Becca and Nora (with whom I'd graduated to a constrained form of niceties, as in "oh-my-gosh-that-skirt-looks-so-good-on-you" or "do-you-have-an-extra-piece-of-bubble-gum"), I was one of General Bullmoose's "secretaries," and this was how we dressed. The role was rewritten for four girls instead of four men, since the men around here were habitually scarce.

From the hall, I could hear two off-pitch voices singing on stage. An actor flubbed his lines, a girl fell short of her high C. My head throbbed. I still had about fifteen minutes before my next scene.

Someone almost ran into me, and I stumbled into the side door that led to the gymnasium balcony. No one would see me here, or so I thought.

I closed my eyes and listened to the squeak of the varsity boys' rubber soles against the vinyl floor, the thwap of the basketball passing from one pair of hands to the next. The blunt clang of the ball hitting the rim, the swift crack of skilled hands dribbling down the court. It was the best music I'd heard in a long time. A symphony in dribbles and missed shots. My head began to clear.

Because I'd broken up with Pete, a beloved Mercury boy, I was becoming known as a girl with a cold heart. It didn't bother me all that much—I'd rather be known as coldhearted than as a girl who was damaged goods. What *did* bother me was whether it was true. I'd lost two of my closest friends, and I couldn't help wondering if there was anything alive left in me. I felt the chill of growing up and growing apart, and I thought I needed a beacon to shine down on me and warm what had frozen.

Boys were never more romantic than when they played basketball. The way their feet felt the floor, the way their hands made sound. Such poetic stallions. They courted the ball, watched it, chased it. Played with it, cradled it, shielded it. Fought for it. What tender fingers extended from such forceful arms. A speaking grip: *This ball is mine, and no one else's.* Oh, to be that ball, to quicken his pulse. To be so round, snug between a set of palms. To be the object of affection, to move, and to be moved by, so many.

The previous spring I decided to try out for the cheerleading squad, and I'd made it. I thought then that I wanted nothing more than for Pete to see me perform in another short skirt. I'd resigned my job as the basketball team's bookkeeper, and watching these boys play, I realized I'd made a mistake that couldn't be undone. I gave up something I loved for another opportunity to exhibit myself for a crowd. An Appalachian Vanity Fair, that's what all this was—the football games, the school plays, the basketball court. It was everywhere, and I was just another antiheroine submitting to its fancies.

I hooked my legs onto the metal pipe at the lip of the balcony. Simon Tierney, a steely-eyed senior and star of the team, turned his head upward and spied me. Simon's father, Mr. Tierney, had been one of the first to confront Mr. Lotte before the rumors had started to swell. Now, five years later, Simon was one of the most popular boys in school. Athletic prowess would always trump any other kind of misdeed in Mercury. Simon's sister Aria was a year behind me in school, and a remarkable athlete in her own right. If anyone thought about the Lotte scandal when they saw Simon or Aria, they didn't dare mention it. Even thinking of it would require facing a difficult truth, and none of us had the courage to face down such a beast.

Simon and I eyed each other for a few moments before the whistle blew again and the basketball boys started a new drill. I tiptoed back toward the stairwell to get in place for my next scene. When I opened the doorway into the hall, I got smacked again with off-key music.

I joined the other secretaries backstage as the tech crew readied some props and the lights went black. Soon, opening night would be over and we'd perform a Saturday night show, then a Sunday matinee. Then, in the wake of musical season, basketball would become the latest object of our affections. As I waited in the dark, I could only see the faint glitter of material at my waist. I thought about Simon, how he observed me with unveiled curiosity. Later, he would tell me it was the glint of my sequin belt that caught his eye, the look of my legs stretched on the balcony railing that kept his attention.

The scene: a varsity basketball game held in some old, small gym in some old, small town, one where fans waited in line to get their hands stamped in exchange for flimsy red ticket stubs. A concession stand set up camp in the hallway where members of the basketball boosters club filed dollar bills in envelopes and kept the change in a canning jar. Everyone in town attended; no one dared miss such an affair. It happened this Friday, or last Friday, or three weeks from Friday. This was one night of many, many nights.

7:48 p.m. Like a league of marionettes, the pep band hopped to attention when the band director flicked his wrist. The pregame entertainment, Bill Haley's "Rock Around the Clock," had remained the same as far back as I could remember. A cheerleading cohort, of which I was the first, flooded the court and formed a double line along the center.

Just before the opening song, the basketball team gathered in the wings, ready for their cue. While waiting, the crowd swapped titillated murmurs until the show began.

When it did, the audience quieted as the pep band counted us in by the numbers on a clock.

One Two Three Four

Shaking our pom-poms, the cheerleaders popped their hips to the side.

Five Six Seven Eight

We kept shaking, bopping as the music swelled.

Nine Ten Eleven Twelve

Here it came—the grand entrance that would never change.

The dewy-skinned basketball boys tore through a sign hung in front of the locker room door and burst onto the court. The line of athletes swarmed around the girls, dazzling the crowd with their practice layups, jump shots, and rebounds. Each player had his moment of presentation to the adoring audience; he whipped off his warm-up pants and tossed them on the bleachers, some of the snaps left undone to assist with the theatrics. The boys shot and scored as the girls primped and pranced. This, a film reel of young dukes and duchesses performing at high court.

7:56 p.m. The pep band slogged through "The Star Spangled Banner." Up in the balcony, Yutes—the waifish school nurse—perched on a metal folding-chair throne, primed to scold any ruffian who forgot to remove his hat for the anthem. Heads bowed and children fidgeted until the final notes resolved.

8:00 p.m. The two opposing centers met in the middle of the court. These were my favorite moments, the athletes itching to go like racehorses. They crouched; the whistle blew. The referee threw the ball in the air, and for a moment it suspended, a dirty orange orb that drew every eye to itself. (A moment here for Mr. Howard Lotte, who had once been that dirty orb that had lured the Mercury flock: where was he on this night, last Friday night, or the one before? Alone in front of his television just a stone's throw from the high school, no longer permitted to attend any school functions? Surely, he entered no one's thoughts but his own.)

Someone from one team or the other snatched the ball and the point guard signaled the first play of the game. For quarters one and two, the eager cheerleaders were relegated to the bleachers. I sat wherever there was a spot, never on the end next to the players. Pete, now a key teammate, had worked his way to the front of the line. The time clock wound down as we offered a few cheers (RED HOT, our team is RED HOT), while someone banged a megaphone against the floor. A few of us performed a rather stout and underwhelming mount in the corner, one girl (a flyer, she was called) balanced on the bent thighs of two girls acting as the base. The flyer's arms shot out at forty-five-degree angles as we shouted, "GO STANGS!"

During practice earlier in the season, I had declined the opportunity to grace the top of the Mustang cheerleader mounts. I was afraid of heights. "Come on," one of the veteran cheerleaders had urged me. "Don't you wanna fly?" I *did* want to fly, but I didn't dare. I knew that falling always came with it.

At halftime, the girls rose to take center stage. The pep band started to play "Centerfold," and the cheerleaders performed a local favorite, coined the "s" dance. Each year, the older girls taught it to the younger. The pep band popped out the loud notes as young, feminine hips gyrated to the tempo. Executed at every home game, everyone knew this was the "s" dance, and everyone knew the "s" was short for slut.

Fans stood and stretched, kibitzed and milled. The girls began an eight-count step that started with hair tousling, as if washing soap suds from our wet manes. We completed it by bending over at the waist, parading our backsides to the visitors' section. *Picture me in the shower*, the choreography demanded. *Picture me bending over.*

But such seduction was never for the basketball boys, the boys who loved their mothers, met their curfews, and always put on wool caps before going outside. The boys who—at this very moment—sat one floor below in a damp locker room and listened to their coach. "This is your moment," he told them. "You better go out there and take it."

Instead, the girls danced for a town made of ghosts. Fathers who used to sit in the locker room, years ago. Mothers who once performed the same "s" dance in the same uniforms. All of Mercury lapped up the display along with saccharine cups of diet pop and melting Hershey's bars, the same town that had railed against seven young girls trying to protect their own integrity once their innocence was taken. The cheerleading squad was filled with Lotte's former students, and we danced for the crowd, but would never even think of doing anything unholy in the backseat of a boy's car. On every bleacher, there was at least one little girl who would grow up and fall in line, just as I had. She was one girl of many, many girls.

⌡

How quickly our town will return to its droll routine of high school pageantry after Mr. Lotte's scandal is tied with a firm bow. But the year of Mr. Lotte's investigation feels like the longest year in Mercury history, and we swear time passes more slowly here than it does anywhere else in America. Just when we get wind of new trends like hyper-color T-shirts and slap bracelets, the rest of the country has already moved on to a new fad. By the time of Lotte's August sentence hearing, the town has grown impatient. He's pled guilty out of the kindness of his heart, so can't someone wrap this up already? Don't you know that peewee football season is just around the corner, and where there is peewee football, there must be peewee cheerleaders, decorated in itchy wool sweaters and bright rhinestone studs in newly pierced ears? There are future Mercury stars and starlets in the making here, and the clock is ticking.

Almost a year after he first confronted Mr. Lotte, Mr. Tierney takes the stand. He doesn't reveal what he said to Mr. Lotte on his front stoop that day, nor what Mr. Lotte said in return, only that he was "unsatisfied with his explanation." What was a father to do? Like Jonah in the belly of the whale, Mr. Tierney waited three days and three nights before deciding to speak. In less than a week, he'd become a Mercury prophet set to deliver a message no one would want to hear.

Mr. Tierney is a bit of a small-town legend himself. Lithe and wiry, he once worked in the Juniper steel mills before they closed and he began a second career in education. He's almost super-human, though more in the manner of Peter Parker than Bruce Wayne. Town lore insists Mr. Tierney once fell off his own roof while cleaning the gutters, only to stand straight up, crack his back, and climb back up to finish the job. He built his own garage, mows his expansive lawn early in the day, and you can count on him to say exactly what he means.

"There was only one choice," he says from the stand during his testimony. "If we didn't come forward, it would send a message to Aria that, if violated, you count your losses, run, and let others fend for themselves."

Though his son Simon will grow into an athletic dynamo in a few years and rescue his parents and sister from being known only as "that family" that started this whole thing, for now Mr. Tierney thinks of his daughter.

> Aria told the truth as she was taught. Her reward has been interviews with three government agencies, necessary but very painful. Aria has been confronted both in and out of school by classmates, accused of lying and being a troublemaker. She has spent nights awakened by nightmares about Mr. Lotte and fears of reprisal. Our family has been treated as criminals, shunned, ridiculed and accused of conspiracy. For what? For taking the appropriate, lawful steps to stop a very

real danger. We didn't make the decision to prosecute but only supplied facts to the respective authorities.

I have been told that the offenses were not serious enough to be of concern, that they were exaggerated. Some may think touching private parts under all clothing is not that bad, but they weren't sitting up nights with a weeping, trembling ten-year-old child. One person even suggested that Aria suffered more going through the legal system than at the hands of Mr. Lotte. When she lay awake unable to sleep, her words were fear of Mr. Lotte and anger at what Mr. Lotte had done, not of the legal system.

His final words resound with the common sense that Mercury in all its hysteria has thrown overboard. "This is not an anti-Lotte issue," Aria's father says. "This is a pro-child issue."

After Mr. Tierney concludes and another parent testifies, Layne Richter's mother takes her turn speaking on her daughter's behalf. She is the wife of a church elder, and though most of the people in town know who she is, they've never heard her voice.

"I don't know if I can be heard," she says after she's sworn in. "I know I speak softly."

Though we aren't there to see her on the stand, there's one thing we know—her eyes are a vision no one in the courtroom will be able to forget. They are the bluest blue, an original-sin-blue, the kind that reminds us how far we've fallen. Her words do the same.

"This situation has pitted friend against friend, teacher against colleague, Christian against Christian, and perhaps most sadly, child against child."

Child against child. Is that the cost of keeping a secret, paid by those who told the truth? It's a penance that makes us sick to collect, and like little, dainty dogs, we return to our vomit.

The *town*, the insidious perpetrator that Mr. Tierney and Mrs. Richter address, will never be put on trial, never be brought to justice, and will never make amends. And why should it? These are just *girls*, after all. We'll bounce back. We're young, for now. Besides, an entire town hasn't come to judgment since the days of Moses and the Old Testament. The difference between Nineveh and Mercury is singular: Nineveh repented when Jonah delivered his message, and Mercury did not.

Audition

IN LATE SPRING OF MY SOPHOMORE YEAR, Simon appeared on my periphery. When I noticed him sliding his eyes toward me when I walked past his physics class, door open, him seated in the last row ("You looked good in those Levis," he later told me), I only let my glance linger a moment before moving on. Even if I wanted him, I could never say it. This was how girls auditioned for boys in Mercury: you strutted, you smiled, and you pretended not to care.

Despite his eye wandering in my direction, everyone in town knew that Simon had always loved that year's homecoming queen, Cara Richter. Though he tried to conceal it, everyone still knew, just like everyone knew which basketball ref wouldn't officiate Saturday night games because he was a Seventh-day Adventist, or that throat cancer had rendered the town dentist unable to speak above a whisper. During routine checkups, he scolded his patients when they reciprocated his soft tone. "You don't have to whisper just because I do," he would say. We were just trying to be polite.

Simon was also known for being a king of grand gesture, and the first I experienced was on Cara's behalf, not mine. Cara's younger sister Layne had become a close friend of mine in the past year since I'd lost Nora and Pete. In their absence, Layne had appeared, somehow implicitly aware of how lonely I was. If anyone understood what it felt like to suddenly find herself alone, it was Layne. It was as if her daring to speak the truth about Mr. Lotte had imprinted kindness on her, an ability to sense the innate needs of others.

When word of the allegations against Mr. Lotte first broke, many of the townsfolk busied themselves by foretelling what would become of the girls who had dared to speak out. They'd be lost, surely. Outcasts. Drunks. Sluts. Jezebels. Now, five years later, not one of their predictions had come true. Instead, Layne was no longer bound by the secret she didn't know we shared, the same secret that still threatened to shrivel me from the inside out.

A year older and a starter on the girls' basketball team, Layne didn't see me much outside of Sundays at Pure Heart Presbyterian. I was drawn to Layne's quiet strength. She wasn't weak, and she wasn't proud—Layne embodied everything I felt I was missing, or perhaps still had burning inside me that was desperate to find an escape. Just by befriending me, she had finally taught me it was possible for one girl to save another, instead of always turning her back.

When I arrived at Layne's house on a Saturday afternoon in late April, all was dark and silent. I crossed the lawn, dotted with a few leftover leaves from last fall. I rang the doorbell and Rilo, the family dog, yelped from somewhere inside. I peered through the glass into the dark foyer where a piano sat, pressed against the side of a staircase. I'd never heard her play. Once so eager to exhibit, most of the girls in town didn't play piano anymore. When I sat at the piano bench, I felt like an impostor, but not because I didn't know how to play. It was because I hadn't told the truth.

When Layne came to the door, she leaned past me and inspected the sparse oncoming traffic.

"Quick," she whispered. "Come inside."

I followed her into the house, creeping through their front room and the kitchen before we huddled on the loveseat in their family room. The television blipped in the corner. The house smelled as it always did, the faint scent of freshly baked Communion bread.

"What's going on?" I asked.

Layne leaned in. "Simon is waiting for Cara in her bedroom."

"Her bedroom?" The birth of a new fantasy simmered beneath my skin. I could picture it—returning home to a darkened house and entering my bedroom to find a benevolent intruder. Things like that never happened in Mercury.

"What's he doing up there?" I asked.

"He's going to ask her to the prom," Layne whispered. "Isn't that romantic?"

I nodded. The moment turned too hallowed for speaking. Simon was directing the show this time, and I, for once, was a member of the hushed audience.

Layne and I watched the muted television as we waited for Cara to return from volleyball practice. The back of my neck tingled as I imagined the scene about to unfold. An unsuspecting Cara would slog up the stairs toward her bedroom. When she crossed the doorframe and tossed her bag on the floor, she'd notice a pair of men's flip-flops next to it. Her gaze would rise, her pupils adjusting to the afternoon light streaming in from the window. Simon's expectant face would overtake her vision, his head of thick hair appearing golden in the shafts of light. She'd take a step back, look behind her, and furrow her gentle brow.

He'd extend his hand, holding a single rose, and pose his question. She'd accept, both the rose and his offer. Then he'd whisk past her, telling her he had somewhere else to be, as all bad boys did.

Afloat in my own imagination, I jumped at the squeak of the front door. Layne squeezed my arm. Silent, we watched each other as we listened to Cara's feet tap up the steps.

Layne and I could hear nothing as we waited. Was Simon still up there? I pictured him again. Was he standing or sitting? Leaning against the vanity, the mirror showcasing the muscles in his back?

After a few minutes dragged by, sound returned. Cara bounded down the steps, through the kitchen and into the family room, red rose in hand.

"Simon really knows how to make an impression," she said, flopping on the couch.

Unable to contain myself, I finally spoke.

"Dude," I said. "*Dude.*"

"Fer-rill," Layne added.

"Is he still here?" I asked.

"No," she sighed. "He left."

Simon had been so close, but I'd not seen him come or go. No evidence of his presence, aside from the rose, remained. Layne and I regarded Cara from the loveseat as she unmuted the television. It wasn't envy I felt, but awe at the magic in her that had inspired such romance.

Desire for Simon, this peculiar phantom, overtook me. I told myself it didn't matter that he wanted someone else, that in time, I could change his mind. Everyone in Mercury was so guarded, but not Simon. He was in love with Cara, who didn't love him back, and still he didn't care who knew. In Simon, I found the kind of unabashed openness that I wanted for myself. I hoped someone with his bravery could expel the fear that crippled me, the one thing I had to conquer if I had any chance of getting out of Mercury.

Simon made his first move during the last week of school before summer break. Each year, the school newspaper released a special edition dedicated to the graduating class. An integral part in the ritual of senior departure, the issue operated as last rite for those bound for a better place, another place, or the same place.

The paper included a feature titled "the senior wills" where the departed bequeathed their belongings to those left behind. Like many of Mercury's customs, these soliloquies obeyed unspoken rules. In bestowing their few belongings, seniors turned regular items to talismans: matchbooks, pom-poms, car keys. Never any rings, necklaces, or heirlooms—nobody liked a showboater. Those weren't the things that mattered anyhow.

A few well-worn bequests:

1. The Inside Joke
   —To Meredith, I leave a trip to the porta-potty on Station Road.
   —To Bobbers, the blue chair in Mr. Ellis's science class, and a pen to go with it. Hee hee.
2. The Maudlin Goodbye
   —To Tim, every bit of deep-down confidence you need to realize what an incredible person you are. Keep spreading your light.
   —Abby, cherish these years. Don't let them slip through your fingers. They disappear too quickly.
3. The Backhanded Gift, aka The Sneaky Sideways:
   —To Shelley, my boyfriend's phone number, since I heard you wanted it.
   —To Chet, another year in remedial math. I hope you pass this time.
4. The Minimalist Approach
   —I leave nothing to no one.

An odd quiet spread throughout the halls of Mercury High School on the day the teachers dispensed the year's final issue during the last period of the day. Students lolled at lockers, some crouching, seeking cover. Pages turned, eyes scanned, mouths grinned. Part of the high came from devouring the issue, hunting for your own name in print, perhaps uncovering a long-concealed crush. I hadn't expected anyone to leave me anything.

Simon and I hadn't interacted much beyond delayed glances in the hallway and my hand brushing his while passing the offering plate on Sunday morning. Hungry for details about him, I read Simon's will first. I squeezed the handle of my locker when I saw Simon had reserved a sincere moment for me:

To Amy Burns, I leave nothing because you are perfect the way you are.

My body felt aflame and my skin flushed as the kids around me pulled from their trances. Lockers slammed shut, voices called to one another. The rush I felt rivaled the one I had when I learned I'd been chosen to be editor of the school newspaper the following year. My stomach contracted, my fingers went cold. Perfectly crafted into an *almost* compliment, Simon's statement had a live edge, so that when given, it cut a little, too. I read it over and over later that night, dissecting it and putting it back together again.

Reading Simon's words gave me a smolder, a sign of life inside my crumbling cask of a heart. The sensation led me to believe he possessed the power to cure my illness.

Picture this: my body on a trampoline, brown hair floating and gleaming, dressed with golden highlights. The scene—Simon's front lawn, all the guests at his graduation party shuffling back and forth from the food to the constellation of card tables. The yard was stuffed with people. I came with my parents because Simon knew everyone; *everyone* here knew everyone.

The trampoline, wide and black with blue skirting, stood shunted to the side, not far from the mass of cars, most of them American-made. When I arrived, I'd intended to shoot straight for the party's nucleus, the head of the snake, and insert myself there. Simon would have to notice me then.

But the trampoline waylaid me, lounging in disuse while a few small children shyly felt its legs. The need to jump—to fly—gripped me as it never had during my short season as a cheerleader.

"Hey," I said, bending toward a little girl circling the tramp's perimeter. "You wanna fly?"

She giggled and turned her head to the side, bashful. I hoisted her up, setting her on top of the springs before kicking off my sandals. It was hot that day, and the grass caught in the trampoline's shadow felt cool on my feet. After pulling myself up, I asked her if she wanted to play popcorn. She did.

"Tuck yourself into a ball," I told her. "Wrap your arms around your legs and don't let go."

We set out, timid at first, a few light jumps that lifted her bottom inches from the bouncing pad. Soon we started to jump high, she and I, opposing forces. She flew when I landed, the nylon stretching and giving way beneath my feet. My pressing down propelled her upward. We both reached higher and higher, tossing each other in the air. She squealed with delight, hiccupping as she landed. The fear of falling no longer grounded me. After a year of wondering whether there was any hope left for me, a resounding *YES* thumped in my chest.

"Hold on," I said. "I think we can get you higher."

I dug into my landing. Sweat streaked through my hair. Higher now, higher. Our speed quickened as we turned jagged circles around each other. Just a little higher now. And there, finally. She flew. *Really* flew, her body limned in sky. We collapsed, giggling and staring upward. I sat up, and the world righted itself. The party still blazed on. Simon, from the heart of the herd, looked back at me.

I was my own solar system, this little girl my moon, needing nothing at all, just as Simon had said.

The following Saturday, Simon picked me up in his old jeep. The jeep was an extension of Simon himself, clean but rugged, primed for adventure. It purred in response to Simon's hand on the stick shift. As we left my neighborhood and crested the hill near town, we sank back for just a moment at the light before hopping forward.

On an early evening in early summer, we rode with the windows down. The breeze had a sublime chill. It felt almost as good as a summer's virgin dive in the Silver Pulley pool, which I hadn't done for two years. With Simon at the wheel and my feet propped on his dashboard, lost sensations bloomed in my stomach. Hope, maybe. Or fear. I couldn't quite distinguish the two. Either way, I was finally heading somewhere.

We waited in line outside the movie theater, and Simon bought us tickets to see *Shine*, starring Geoffrey Rush. We chose a pair of seats that creaked as we settled in. I sat to his right, and Simon rested his right ankle on his left knee so that our knees met.

When the lights faded, the speakers crackled like bacon in a frying pan. The film strip blinked. From the opening scene, the plot arrested Simon. He scooted forward in his chair and buckled over during the few funny parts, slapping my knee as he struggled to compose himself. His laugh flooded the theater. He clutched the chair's armrest as the drama heightened, each fingernail stunted by an aggressive biting habit.

When the movie ended, Simon collapsed against the back of his chair. The abandon with which he viewed the film left him both exhausted and invigorated. Sitting beside him in an old, forgotten theater, I started to shed the parts of myself I thought were holding me back. I could be bold, defiant, and what I'd always wished to be but never quite was—steel-hearted. For the first time, I felt sexy because I felt like someone else.

"There's nothing sexier," Simon told me as we drove through town in his jeep, "than a girl who can drive a stick."

I took my feet off the dashboard and sat up. An awkward pause swelled between us. I couldn't drive a stick. Simon knew I couldn't drive a stick. It was early July, and I was auditioning for him, still.

Simon tapped the steering wheel as we pulled to a stop across from an old, fenced-in graveyard. The jeep hummed.

"And if she's driving in a pair of cowboy boots," Simon added, "I'd be down for the count."

I frowned. As if we were a pair of actors cast and recast in a series of films, Simon vacillated between moments of acute desire for my attention and an urgent need for me to realize that this thing between us was nothing more than ephemeral. One day, he'd put on the bad-boy persona, a kid from the wrong side of the tracks who catches the pretty young thing's eye. The next, he'd turn into an alchemic brooder, leaving me out of it. And my least favorite character was the paternalistic Simon. Not long after our first kiss, he told me how much he loved the song "Crash Into Me" by the Dave Matthews Band. When I told him I loved the song too, he recoiled. Simon's attraction to me stemmed from his vision of a virginal girl, wholly untouched, and he didn't want the truth messing with it. It wasn't me he was drawn to, but his casting of me in his mind.

"You shouldn't listen to that stuff," he'd said. "That song is dirty."

"Don't tell me what music I can and can't listen to," I shot back.

Simon made me angrier than anyone I'd ever met, but I gave him my forgiveness so often because he knew how to ask for it.

"You're absolutely right," he'd said. "I'm sorry."

I looked out the window. The light turned green. Simon shifted gears, and the jeep jumped forward. As the air moved through the windows, the tension dissipated. Though Simon's riddles often left me confused, I relished the challenge, each interchange a spar for one of us to gain prowess over the other.

"You know I like you, right?" he said.

There it was, everything I wanted—his shimmering honesty and his disregard for the consequences of it.

"I like you, too," I answered.

"You do?"

"I thought it was obvious."

Simon smiled. "Just one thing, though."

The engine idled. I grew nervous.

"I don't like the suitcases," he said.

"The suitcases?"

"Yeah, you know. The baggage. I don't want it."

"Oh," I said.

"I'm leaving for college soon," he said. He planned to study engineering at a university close to Erie, a little under an hour away.

I sighed. "You think I don't know that?"

Though this sentiment hadn't surprised me, the words stung. I had thought his capacity for bold truths had drawn me to him, but these quick moments of honesty did nothing but repel us. We were better at playacting truth than we were at honoring it.

As we merged onto the highway, a thrashing wind filled the jeep. Simon sulked, and I fiddled with a strand of my hair. How quickly the mood had darkened.

Simon and I shared just one secret that summer, a confidence that tumbled out sideways during another car ride on another sunny afternoon. We were cruising around town, and we passed the courthouse where Mr. Lotte's trial had been held five years earlier. The scandal had been buried without any apologies offered, and the town was still sick with some disease, still caught between amnesia and dumbness of the mouth. *We need to put this behind us*, people had said. *For the sake of our community.* But silence hadn't been the antidote everyone had hoped it would be.

I thought of Mr. Lotte every time I passed that spot, an area known around town as "the diamond" for the way the streets crisscrossed around the courthouse. This was Mercury: a place I loved more than any other, a town where diamonds were only landmarks, a stretch of earth where it never seemed to thunder and lightning at the same time. Yes, I remembered Mr. Lotte, though I never pictured the two of us together. His face and body had turned amorphous in time, leaving behind a bitterness whose genesis I—still in my fugue state—could not determine.

As Simon and I rode past the courthouse, his eyes hazed. Shifting gears, he took a left turn and accelerated.

"I hate Mr. Lotte," he said.

So skilled at keeping my own secrets, especially from myself, I said nothing. Still, Simon had my full attention. He pulled over to the side of the street and turned toward me.

"If I ever do anything that makes you uncomfortable, you have to tell me," he said. His expression and tone were almost violent with urgency.

"You never make me uncomfortable," I said.

"No." Simon was insistent. "You have to promise me."

"I promise," I said. "I'll tell you."

Simon could never make me feel fear in the way Mr. Lotte still had the power to. I saw him just once after the trial. He was walking through town with his wife. Just walking through town, not far from the courthouse, not far from where Simon and I now sat. That's how it was in Mercury—your greatest joys occurred in the same spots as your worst secrets, and often it was impossible to distinguish one from the other.

The day I saw Mr. Lotte, I rode in the backseat of my father's car, headed in the same direction as he was, and I recognized the back of his head. When I saw him, shock coursed through my body, and it felt just like that day I sat on his piano bench and his hands began to wander. Instinct caused me to slouch in my seat, and we passed him by. Then I sat up, puzzled by how swiftly my body executed a command my brain did not give.

The regret of an untold secret was a merciless captor. How long I'd kept it, despite so many opportunities for release. Even Carly and I spoke about Mr. Lotte's investigation only once while sitting in the last row of chairs after a Sunday church service. Side by side we sat, both in tights and buckled shoes.

She didn't ask if Mr. Lotte ever touched me, and she didn't ask whether I believed her. Of course I did. As a child, I was able to believe it had happened to her while denying that it had happened to me. Carly shifted toward me in her chair.

"Right after church today, I went into the hallway to get a drink of water at the fountain." Her chin quivered. "You know Ricky Flagg?"

I nodded. Ricky Flagg was a kid about our age who went to our school. He liked to draw pictures and throw rocks.

"I stood behind him in line at the fountain, and when he was done drinking, he turned around and said, 'I know what you did. I know all about you.'"

I didn't need to ask, but I did anyway. "He was talking about Mr. Lotte?"

She nodded. "He thinks I'm a liar."

My stomach twisted.

Carly rubbed her eyes. "I ran into the kindergarten classroom so he wouldn't see me cry."

"He's just a jerk, Carly." I felt my own tears beginning to form. "A stupid jerk."

She sniffed. I just stared at her, unsure what else to do.

"Wait here," I said. "Just wait."

Planning to find Ricky, I ran to the hallway where the water fountain was. "Stay away from my friend," I was going to tell him. "Or else." "You leave her alone," I'd say.

But by the time I got to the hallway, it was empty and the lights had been shut off. Ricky Flagg was long gone, and my attempt to make pathetic amends was thwarted.

Now, more than five years later, this memory was just one of many that built a barrier between me and anyone who dared attempt to breach it. Simon stared at me in earnest, as if trying to pull out an unrevealed truth not about me, but about himself.

"Simon," I said again. "You never make me uncomfortable."

He sighed. A few cars rushed past, and Simon turned on the left signal before merging back onto the road. We never talked about it again.

♪

While Mr. Lotte waits to receive his punishment, those of us who stayed silent concern ourselves with parties and posing for photographs. We've graduated into the age of serial sleepovers and our first boy-girl parties, and we're running wild with excitement. Hungry for a new sensation, we fantasize. Our little minds let us travel not beyond Mercury's borders—our imaginations can't reach that far—but beneath them, into other basements besides Mr. Lotte's, into slow dances that crackle like the radio, into letting a boy sip from our plastic cups of orange soda next to a hanging bike rack and a dusty pile of free weights, into knowing what it's like to stay out until ten o'clock at night. Oh, the fever it causes, and we are aching to get sick.

At every sleepover, we spend the first few hours in our pajamas posing in front of a Polaroid camera, pretending to be models.

"You totally could become a model in New York if you want," we take turns saying to each other.

"We're gonna do it," says the shortest girl in our class. "Guaranteed."

One girl wears sunglasses, a tight royal blue nightshirt and rainbow-striped tights. We all fawn over her tights and beg to borrow them. Another wears a XXL Paul Mitchell shirt that her mom got for free at a hair salon. It drags on the floor and her head can fit through the armholes. We pass around glittered Chapstick and headbands, pairs of sunglasses and cheap neon nail polish. We act like we're posing for the click of the camera, tossing our hair and pouting our lips, but the camera is just a piece of plastic that allows us to continue doing what we do best—pose for each other.

After a while, we get bored with the Polaroid photos and start to chat. It begins with the normal things: boys we like, girls we don't, summertime madness, and school-time blues. We spread out across the living room, legs slung on recliners and couch arms, bodies sprawled across the carpeted floor. But as we talk, we start to inch toward each other. We speak so softly that our faces end up in a bunch so that we can hear.

"Do you think he's gonna go to jail?" someone asks.

"No way," one of us says.

"Sure, he is. I'd bet money on it," says someone else.

No one needs to identify who "he" is or what "he" did. Lotte's former students never say a word, as silence is our method of survival. The other girls titter and gasp, and we listen with attention until someone's mother sweeps in from the kitchen.

"Girls!" she speaks sternly. "What is this dirty talk?"

We all look to the floor and remain silent.

"I don't want to hear another word. Do you hear me?"

We all nod, and the mother exits the room more slowly than she entered. She shuts the glass door that leads to their piano room—almost every home in Mercury has one. We can see it from the couch. No longer in use, the piano bench is covered with papers and magazines. Even the metronomes have gone silent, but their ghostly ticking lives on in the faces of wristwatches and the blinking lights of airplanes passing overhead. *Tock tock tock tock.* Piano benches across town wait for someone to sit on them, but no one is playing piano in Mercury.

For a few minutes we sit in silence before someone finally starts taking pictures again. No talking. We put on pairs of sunglasses and smile for the camera.

At boy-girl parties, talking is encouraged. Boys will be boys, and boys will be rowdy. They arrive in packs, spreading themselves throughout the basement in awkward clumps of sneakers and fresh haircuts. They smell like Downy and grass, as if all their basketball tournament T-shirts were first tumbled dry and then hung outside on the clothing line. The girls pair up to approach them, or go solo, if they dare.

The heavenly night stretches before us as we spy the cherry-red lips of every boy in the basement. If you think girls have the reddest, softest lips, surely you've never seen the boys we know in Mercury. Looking at their buoyant faces, their ruddy cheeks, their sweating palms, we start to think that this is where safety resides. Our best bet is to find one boy to take shelter within, and we'll do our best to find a nice one. Not a fickle one like the girls we know and know ourselves to be. When the time comes to play spin the bottle, it's enough for us to just knock knees with the boys on either side as we all sit cross-legged in a circle. The empty two-liter pop bottle bucks beneath the force of eager wrists. It spins like a racing disco ball, catching the spark of the bright yellow tube lights above us.

Kissing one boy, two boys, three boys, four. Sometimes it's just his mouth that touches us, other times we can feel the easy weight of his fingertips on our slender collarbones. It's the innocence we love, the illusion of danger without the threat of it, the faint taste of orange pop on our lips when we pull away. We've already started to pretend that *this* is danger, or perhaps we never stopped.

Soon, the braver, bustier girls will challenge a boy to make out with her while someone times them with a watch. *See*, she seems to be able to say with her mouth without using any words. *See how far I will go?*

But none of us good girls would ever dream of going that far, so we sit on the couch away from the action, or wait at the window for the coming headlights of our parents' cars. The clock is about to strike ten, and our time with the Rust Belt cowboys will be over for the night. Still, we can't help but be mystified by these brash girls, so un-ashamed of their youthful sexiness, able to French-kiss a boy and not think twice about it. We can't help but wonder—if we ever went that far, or farther—what kind of girl, then, would we be?

Underststudy

ON A JULY EVENING that felt like afternoon, I spent my sweet sixteen in a cemetery. It was Simon's idea, and I knew by then not to question him. Each time I saw him, he'd fashioned another temporary escape route for the two of us—he, the mastermind, and I, the fledgling actress. I wanted to convince him I could embody his darkest ideas. Throw something at me and see if I flinch.

"I want to go someplace quiet," he explained while we were en route. He stuck a freckled hand out the window of the jeep, and his palm bucked against the wind. As was our custom, we said little. Often we spent car rides without speaking, the open windows and wind providing the noise we needed for silence between us.

"Hey," he said as he slowed to a stop sign. "Are you afraid of cemeteries?"

"Nah," I lied.

When we turned down a thin, dirt road that led to a small cemetery, I started to feel nervous.

"Sorry I spoiled the surprise," he said as he pulled to a stop.

Even after a month together, my heart still surged at hearing his voice on the phone or seeing the jeep pull around the curve in front of my house. Simon, *the* Simon, had done all this for the eager girl he saw in me, the girl with so much promise who just needed to be shaped.

He handed me a thin bedsheet for us to sit on, and he grabbed his mother's wicker picnic basket out of the back of the jeep. I followed him down the narrow, dusty path toward a spot skirting the edge of the property. A row of trees rose to our right, a legion of tombstones lay to our left. A myriad of Mercury names chiseled in rock—Burk, Burke, Messer, Husband, Allen, Steingrabe. Names of my classmates, their parents, and their parents' parents. Families, then and now, tangled like vines.

We sat down near the perimeter of stones, and the grass beneath us gathered in tufts. It had just been mown. We took off our shoes.

"Beautiful." Simon said as he leaned back and stretched out his legs. The fair skin on his hands blended with the pale bedsheet, his light eyes squinting at a clear sky.

I didn't want to tell Simon that I'd never been in a cemetery before. I knew he liked a bit of naiveté, but I didn't think he'd like a scaredy-cat. Instead, I focused on the cemetery's geometry, a pattern of crisscrosses, squares, and diamonds, the stones themselves in varying states of decay. If privacy was what Simon wanted, he succeeded. There was no one around, not even an occasional car on the far road. We were alone.

In a skirt for the occasion, I sat with my legs folded tightly beneath me. Sweat pooled behind my knees. At the height of summer, the July sun still hung even in late afternoon. I smiled at Simon and tucked my drooping curls behind my ear.

Opening the flap of the basket, he pulled out a plastic container. Thin driblets of condensation gathered along the rim of the lid.

"Close your eyes," he directed.

I obeyed and heard a pop as he removed the cap. I waited.

"Open," he said.

Inside the container, he'd arranged a fan of cold shrimp around a small bowl of cocktail sauce.

"Do you like shrimp?" he asked.

"Yes," I lied again. I'd never tasted shrimp before, but it seemed like something I should have done already.

I bit into a piece of shrimp, and its gristle ground against my teeth. When I reached the tail, I lingered. When Simon tossed his shrimp tail into a plastic bag, I did the same. Even in these small things, I mirrored him.

We sat, saying very little as the sun sank and a humid dusk settled in. Without any wind or music to mask it, the quiet hung around us like a thick blanket. As the heat let up, I relaxed, and he broke the silence.

"Happy sweet sixteen," he said.

Sixteen, such a candy-coated number. I smiled and ran my fingers through my hair. I leaned toward him, closing my mouth on his. I wanted Simon to remember me cast in this haunting frame: his pretty, young brunette, the wind just catching my hair as the sun set, a bouquet of dead flowers lying limp against a gravestone in the background.

Just before dark, we left the cemetery and headed for Simon's house. He lived a few miles past the high school on the way out of town, in between the cornfields and farms. His house wasn't far from the home of infamous town lore, the farm where a trio of unsolved murders was committed in 1943. Three people killed—one found shot in the stairwell, the other shot in the living room. One more strangled in the barn. There had been a love triangle, an angry farmhand, a rich man who mysteriously skipped town. Now, another family owned the property and raised horses there. Driving past it reminded me of the day Nora and I entered the vacant house on Route 44, a house that now owned the ghost story of the two of us.

I hadn't visited Simon's house much. Most of the time we spent together was spent alone, either in his car or at restaurants, an occasional movie in my parents' basement. He kept me from much of his life—we never went out with his friends, nor did we talk much about his plans for college in the fall. We existed in a deep pocket of time, each encounter an isolated incident free from outside influence. Timeless, you might say, but not forever.

It was dark by the time we pulled into his long driveway. The trampoline I'd jumped on at his graduation party still sat in the same location, off to the side of the house.

"I liked watching you jump on this trampoline," he said. "You looked so . . . young."

"Young?" I repeated. "I'm not that much younger than you. Just two years."

"More like three." He put his arm around my waist. "People might say I'm robbing the cradle, but I don't care."

I didn't argue the point. I knew not to adulterate the very basis of my appeal.

"You wanna jump?" he asked, pointing to the tramp.

I shook my head. "I can't. I'm in a skirt."

He shrugged. "Suit yourself."

Inside the house, I took a seat in his living room. The whole first floor was dark. I knew his parents and his sister Aria were somewhere inside; their cars were in the driveway. I wondered if he'd asked them to stay hidden.

After putting in a video recording of Baz Luhrmann's *Romeo and Juliet* into the VCR, Simon sat down beside me. Close. When the film began, the camera focused in on a brooding Romeo waiting on the beach, a cigarette slipping from his lips as Radiohead sang a jaded melody.

The thought of dying young aroused Simon. I could tell by his breath's urgent rhythm, the rapid tapping of his fingers on the nape of my neck. In the film, Romeo's and Juliet's eyes first met through a glass fish tank. As Romeo and Juliet kissed for the first time, Simon turned my chin toward him. I could see the onscreen lovers out of the corner of my eye as he worked on my lips. He clutched my waist, squeezed his eyes shut, and puckered his brow in fervent concentration. I kept my eyes open. Simon's body gave the appearance of intimacy, but he escaped inside himself as we kissed. It was not my body he sought.

Slowly I pulled away, leaning into my side of the sofa. The bottomless need Simon and I shared had been masquerading as sexual, but the truth was far more insidious. An inescapable vice gripped us both—in the car, at the cemetery, in the movie theater—we both needed to charm the ordinary into the exotic, and we needed each other to do it.

When the film ended, I checked the time. A quarter to midnight. My curfew was twelve.

"Simon," I said. "I have to go."

He turned toward me, and that's when I saw it—something true. *Stay*, his face seemed to say, *Stay. If I fall asleep now, I don't think I'll wake up in the morning. Please. Stay awake with me.*

The ferocity in his eyes frightened me, and yet I couldn't look away. His expression scared me not because it was strange or foreign, but because I recognized it. It was human. It was fear. It was me. As I watched him, I realized I had been fooled by my own reflection. It wasn't only the girls in Mercury who felt trapped. The boys felt trapped here, too.

"Simon," I said again.

He blinked and then started hunting for his shoes.

"Okay," he said. "Let's get you home."

In the minutes before midnight on my sweet sixteen, the night fell cool and quiet as we drove. The subtle terror I felt in his living room eased as the evening wind swept through the car. Surely, we weren't so desperate, the two of us. Not on a beautiful night, not when we were still so young.

"Did you see what I did during the movie?" he asked me, taking his eyes off the road to look into mine. "The way I kissed you?"

"What do you mean?" I asked.

"Like Romeo kissed Juliet."

I paused, trying to remain honest. "I felt like Juliet," I said.

He smiled. "Good."

Yes, I'd felt like Juliet. Every sensation, every gesture with Simon was cinematic. Every tilt of my head, every cock of my brow. "You're incredible," he'd say on the phone, though never to my face. He was teaching me to look underneath the obvious, to seek the longing found in a trembling lip, to sense the curl of his penetrating smile on the back of my neck.

Simon had become a true auteur, rendering our story through the lens of the world as he hoped to find it. Not once did he compromise. And now, I was his eager ingénue, already primed to feel the sharp edge of his profile when he would turn away from me for the last time.

We were broken before we ever began. He wanted to employ me as he saw fit, and fleeting was the half-life of our unequal duet. But even this, I would learn to use. Even as I depended on him, I was learning to look out for myself. Simon, in all his tricks and riddles, was not just preparing me to be left. He was teaching me to leave.

But I was too caught up with Simon, my heartless addiction, to learn the lesson he was trying to impart. Later that summer at camp on Lake Erie, he ignored me for the first five days and nights. His behavior suggested he didn't want Cara, his homecoming dream, to see us together. I refused to ask Simon about it for fear he'd tell me the truth.

On the final night of camp, he decided to take notice of me. I told myself that if he paid me any attention I'd make myself unavailable. The mind was willing, but the heart was weak. When he approached me at the campfire, even as I stood next to Aaron in a crowd of people, desire tempered my resolve, and I found myself unable to say no.

"Let's walk to the beach," he said. I could barely hear him over the din of the fire, the kids, and the waves.

Beside me, Aaron raised his eyebrows. I looked away.

The rocky path leading to the beach was dimly lit, and after escaping the campfire clamor and scrutiny, Simon took my hand as we climbed down the stone trail. When we reached the end of the path, he put his hand around my waist and we sat on the last step of the walkway before the rocky beach hit. Surrounded by litter, driftwood, and dead fish, the water looked dark and beautiful, slick like oil, the light of the moon sliding against it.

Sitting on this beach at night, summer after summer, always put a lump in my throat. Long ago, I'd fallen in love with this place, even though—or perhaps because—it was dirty and rotting and disregarded. This was one of the only places I came where I didn't want to escape myself. I didn't want time to pass, and I didn't ever feel the need to leave. I could turn infinite just by sitting on these blanched rocks, watching the tide come and go, bringing in debris and washing it away.

Beside me, Simon fidgeted. I could tell he wanted to kiss me. He had that look of getting lost in his own head, as he often did before making his move. His mind's eye had already conjured this scene on the midnight beach before he'd asked me to join him. But he said something first.

"Take off your glasses."

I brought my hands to my face. I didn't often wear my glasses because I hated how I looked in them. That night, smoke from the fire had stung my eyes and my contacts had gone dry. Camp, I realized, was the only place I let anyone see me in my glasses.

"Why?" I asked.

"I like you better with your glasses off."

Sudden regret hit me as I lifted the lenses from my face. Complying with his demand felt like an admission of an intimate fault. It had been confessional, my letting him see the girl I kept in my bedroom. With my glasses, I had been naked. Now, with them cast aside, I was clothed again.

"That's better," Simon said as he tucked them in his pocket. "You are so beautiful."

We began the first in a string of vacant kisses. It wasn't me he was kissing, but his starlet, the one he'd imagined. Searching Simon's mouth for some kind of oracle, I found it empty.

I turned away from him for a moment and looked out at the water, though I couldn't see it. I loved the sound of Lake Erie at night, the roar of the waves creeping up the vines on the cliff where others gathered by the fire. The twisted, sun-bleached pieces of driftwood resembled the soft arms of ballerinas extending from the sand.

"You know," Simon said. "Back in school, all those cold winter nights after the basketball games ended, I always went home by myself." The water rushed in. "I just wanted someone to drive home. I hated being alone."

"Me, too." I watched him, almost forgiving him for removing my glasses. His hair looked like copper in the moonlight.

He looked at me. "I wish I'd known you then."

He touched my jawline and kissed me. I wanted to get lost in the moment, lost in him, to find some kind of rush to sustain me through fall, winter, and spring until I'd return here again. Just before I shut my eyes, I heard a rustle of leaves coming from the back trail. I could see the path, thick with trees, from where I sat, and squinted as the figure came into dull focus. Even without my glasses, I could tell that it was Aaron, walking by himself in the dark.

When he saw us, he came to an abrupt stop and his head leaned to the side. I didn't need to make out the features of his face to feel the tilt of his head admonish me: *don't you see what he's doing to you?*

I did see. I was an actress—no, worse—I was Cara's understudy in a romantic memory Simon was filming in his mind. I didn't have the strength to call it what it was. I wasn't what Simon wanted, and no amount of manufactured illusion could change it. I suppressed the realization because it echoed too loudly of the night I found out I wasn't good enough to stay on as one of Mr. Lotte's prized students—the first time a man had ever broken me down so mercilessly.

On the beach, Aaron and I locked eyes, though I couldn't see him well with Simon's face on mine. I watched Aaron's hazy silhouette become a dark blur as he turned around and went back the way he came.

Soon, we grew bored but didn't want to go to bed, not yet. Simon stopped kissing me and we just sat, side by side, as the waves took the beach.

On his last night in town, Simon took me to his favorite Mercury spot, a place called Big Bear not far from the interstate. Though it was one of our town's mythic landmarks, I'd never been there. It was a quiet, sulky night, and the August heat bore down. The trees, bushes, and weeds along the highway seemed to turn away from us as we fled away from town.

The wind thrashed through the jeep's windows as we drove, a little too fast, down the empty stretch of highway. Beside me with eyes straight ahead, Simon ruled the driver's seat. His trusted companion, the jeep always headed somewhere as he delved inward, escaping to places I could not follow.

After we flew down the highway, Simon hooked a strong right turn down a dirt road almost hidden by brush and low-hanging tree branches. He pulled the jeep to a jagged stop and hopped out.

"This is it?" I asked.

"This is it."

Big Bear was a skinny one-lane bridge with a fine trickle of water running beneath it. The road disappeared after the metal siding arced down to the ground. A soft patch of grass lay beyond it, undisturbed.

"Why do people come here?" I asked.

"Just because," he answered. "It's something to do."

"Why is it called Big Bear?"

"Just because."

The dull metal clanged under our feet as we crossed the bridge. We were barely able to see each other, the only light coming from the far-off interstate, I-80 that would take us east to west, and even farther, I-79 that would take us south to Pittsburgh. On the outskirts of the Steel City, the Paris of Appalachia, the earthen point where the tired Monongahela and Allegheny rivers still joined like a tailbone at the rise of a woman's legs, Simon and I stood still, peering down into a sinking crater of mud.

When I'd first met him, I thought Simon and I complemented each other. He had flair; I had poise. He was effervescent where I was reserved. His spontaneity countered my focus, much like Nora's had. But I had never met anyone else whose fears more closely matched my own—we were both scared to death of being bored for the rest of our lives.

We'd never move to California or visit the coast. We'd never start over in New York City, or so we thought. If we wanted to succeed, the sure bet was to stay local. Work in an office of a manufacturing plant. There was good money to be made there, we were told, and tempering our dreams was the only way to fend off inevitable disappointment.

Standing on the bridge, Simon and I tried to say goodbye and failed. He removed an imaginary top hat from his head, bowed, and extended a hand toward me. I took it, and he twirled me beneath his arm. We tried to laugh, but the soggy ground beneath us sucked away the sound.

"Don't forget me," I joked.

He gasped. "Never."

Simon created in me a sensation I couldn't equate to love. It was too hungry and debased for that. He made me feel exhilarating dissatisfaction that led to hot longing, not for him, but for his cinematic recasting of the quotidian into the gothic. Now he was leaving, just when he'd made me his junkie. We remained on the bridge a few moments too long, not holding each other, staring at nothing. I didn't dare ask if he loved me, because I knew that he didn't.

♪

Each year when autumn arrives, the men in western Pennsylvania—our fathers, uncles, teachers, and policemen—rise early to hunt. Find the slick rifle slung next to his thick red-and-black checkered flannel, his bright orange hat and vest caught on the coat hooks by the back door. Smell his coffee brewing in the dark of the kitchen on the first day of buck season. Sit with him as he drinks it—black, as always—before the sun is up.

In the early morning hours, study the premonitory aim of his rifle, cocked in the direction that the buck will dart—an intuition gleaned from seasons spent in these woods, camouflaged with his own father. See how he lowers his gun when a doe with her fawns wanders into his scope, how he watches them in wonder.

Hear the clank of pennies rattling in an empty milk jug as he shakes it at the high school football game on a Friday night. See the tunnels of warm air escape from his mouth and nostrils in the cold. He won't wear gloves. He'll clap his hands together when he's cold or rub them together furiously as if he were starting a fire with a stick. He'll stomp his boots on the metal bleachers when we score a touchdown. He'll accuse the referee of being partial, blind, or worse. He'll pump his fist in the air when the Mustangs win, and he'll huff off to his four-wheel-drive truck when they lose, fuming inside the cab while the engine warms, lamenting that the team just hasn't been the same since he played.

Find him in late afternoon, scraping up the last of the leaves from the dying ground. Watch him dump them on the wet, decaying pile in the backyard. Bum a cigarette from him as he waits for the leaves to be dry enough to catch fire.

Or find one of these men just before autumn, on a sweltering August day, accepting the task of defending Howard Lotte in front of a small-town courtroom and an impartial judge. His client has already pled guilty, and now the attorney sets his sights on helping Mr. Lotte avoid jail time. He appeals to the home crowd and its affection for high school football, the needle that might stitch a severed town back together, the Friday-night bucket that holds all our hopes and dreams.

Coming into this courtroom today, as I was looking outside, it reminded me of attending—and I'll use my high school—a Brighton

High football game. You were either pro-Brighton or against Brighton, the visitors. And I was saddened because I as a lawyer do not represent Mercury; I represent Howard Lotte in this case. And it's true. You've got the pro-Lotte and the anti-Lotte supporters.

The pro-Lotte supporters have demonstrated the greatest character flaw and the greatest character strength, and that's loyalty . . . And then this game that we have, the two sides, the ball that's in the middle of the field really is Howard Lotte and the kids; and the guy that's in the striped shirt is His Honor.

After opening with such a stellar metaphor (really, Lotte as the *ball?*), he goes on to defend his choice of testifying psychologist, a woman who works at the school and is friends with Mr. Lotte. After six sessions together, she states that while he admits to touching his students throughout his twenty years of teaching, he still hasn't admitted that his actions were "for sexual gratification." Surely someone in the courtroom has to wonder what on earth they've been talking about for the past two months.

Either way, the psychologist insists that he needs help, that he's not a typical offender, whatever that means. To her, it means that "as far as incarceration, I do not see how that would serve a purpose; and I think that would be detrimental at this point to his treatment." The transcript starts to read like an intervention on Lotte's behalf, rather than justice on behalf of the seven girls, and his attorney continues to ride the wave.

Howard Lotte has lost everything. The only thing he hasn't lost right now is whatever freedom of mobility that he has. He's lost his jobs, which he resigned for acts that were not occurring in the school. He lost his position at his church, and he lost his career. He doesn't teach piano to anyone.

He claims it's time for the community to recognize reality. What a laughable sentiment to offer to a group of weary parents whose daughters have become public enemies while Mr. Lotte's support fund continues to grow. Those who need to recognize reality most are nowhere near that courtroom; we've scurried down our rabbit holes, and there we'll remain until it's safe to come out. But in a place where Mr. Lotte's welfare is paramount, it may never be safe enough.

In the meantime, the lawyer continues:

> What we have to do, and what I would suggest, is the man has a sickness. He has admitted that. For those of you that are here to support him and are his friends—and most of you are—he has admitted to a lot of people and to you openly in court that he did those acts. And he has never called the children liars; that's evident by the process that he pursued in a guilty plea. If he would have called the children liars, he would have demanded a preliminary hearing, he would have put the children through the rigors of a trial. He did not want, nor did that happen, because those kids were telling the truth.
>
> And on the other side of that coin, on the other side of the football field, he was telling the truth. He could have easily said: I'm not saying anything.

We don't know if Lotte's attorney is a hunter, but here he takes aim and shoots so wide of the mark that all of the girls he just targeted can't help but laugh. And we thought *we* were the naïve ones, just girls who are prone to fantasy. We can attest, more than anyone else, that it's not so easy to say nothing—not so easy at all. No one told us that acts of omission will always age into acts of desertion.

Mirror, Mirror

AFTER I THOUGHT SIMON had disappeared for good, his preoccupation with tragedy left me with a hangover I didn't try to cure. Death's shadow, recondite and pliable, started appearing in unforeseen places. I noticed things I'd ignored before, like the glut of roadkill on Route 17 and the town's omnipresent smell of burning leaves. Each fall, millions of dead leaves were cremated in backyard bonfires and rusty metal drums. The aroma was inescapable.

As a child, I liked to walk in town during the fall, to smell the scent of burning leaves and hear the throb of the bass drum in the distance before a Friday night football game. One last chance to walk through the maze of Victorian houses before a long, cold winter. In the fall, we'd rake leaves, we'd bag them, we'd burn them. The burn pile always caught fire quickly, and my eyes stung from the charred bits of leaves dancing around me like confetti. A yearly communal ritual, raking and burning the dead. A welcome for winter.

Like school, church, and funerals, fires in my town were a community affair. Penn's Auto, Conley's Car Dealership, Rip's Sunrise Market. We all felt the loss when a piece of the commercial landscape disappeared. That's what happens when Rip's is the only grocery store in town. Sometimes the cause was electrical, sometimes it was suspected arson. Other times, suspected insurance fraud.

"They'll rebuild," people liked to say as a way of comforting each other. "They'll rebuild and it'll be just like it was, or even better."

The building's remnants and charred framework would show up on the front page of the local newspaper the following morning next to a picture of what the building used to look like. How we would all remember it.

Memory was this way, too—a community affair. I never got to see any of the buildings burn. I never saw the moment they turned over from *is* to *was*. But you hear enough people talk about it, and somehow it becomes your story, too. The capturing of it, the forgetting of it. The silt that gathered at the dams of our throats.

—*You 'member 'at old auto parts store? It had a backroom full-a-dirty movies. Used to be dahn where the bank is now. I still got three films I rented aht the night it burnt dahn.*

—*Nah. That ain't it. That was Gene's General. Don't you remember anything anymore? Penn's Auto was on the other side of the street.*

—*It was? Nah. Don't believe it. Yer jaggin' me.*

—*Eh, suit yerself. But 'at fire wasn't near as bad as Conley's dillership. Remember 'at one? Propane explosion. Half near the whole tahn was evacuated.*

—*'Course I remember. Hey, they never did rebuild 'at Penn's Auto, did they?*

—*Nope. They never did.*

That year, fall's deathly stupor even infiltrated the stage at Mercury High School, the only arena left for me to feign immortality. I couldn't deny it—my character in *Guys and Dolls*, Great-Aunt Abernathy, was *old*. She hunched when she walked, leaned on a cane, and failed to steady the palsy in her hand. Even the church mission she supported was on its last legs. Save-a-Soul Mission, a withering band of believers outfitted with a brass quartet and a bass drum, trudged through a town full of gamblers, ringing bells and praying to fill the pews of an empty church.

From the moment I landed the role in September, I'd avoided turning myself old. By the time the dress rehearsal arrived in November, the time for waiting to grow old had run out. Standing alone in the hallway bathroom across from the auditorium, I bent over and my long, brown hair fell to the floor like a waterfall. As I showered the underside of my hair with gray paint, an ashen cloud consumed the room. The odor burned my nostrils. Saturated, my head sank toward the tile.

My mother and I had discovered the spray paint in the Halloween aisle at Rite Aid a few weeks ago, next to the fake blood and white face paint.

"I sure don't need any of this," my mother had said in the store, holding the package of hair spray. "Not with my hair."

My mother, though young, had a head of striking white hair. As far back as I could remember, her hair had been salt-and-pepper, even in her late twenties. The pure white suited her; she always looked regal, even in sweat pants. She didn't mind joking about it, either. "You can always find me in a crowd," she liked to say.

Once, when she'd been my age, my mother's hair had been chestnut brown like mine. I'd seen it in her high school photos, her straight hair parted down the middle, the background tinged with an orange glow. Her face and smile remained untarnished; only her hair and the shade of the picture betrayed the time's passing. My mother left her own small hometown in Maine in 1975, and as far as I could tell, she hadn't looked back.

I never understood why I didn't tell my parents the truth about Mr. Lotte. They were confused, like the rest of the town, loath to swallow the reality that they'd left their daughters alone with a pedophile for years' worth of half-hour lessons. All I can say is that Mr. Lotte turned Mercury into a land of opposites: safety turned to danger, truth to lies, and the young turned old. Who could be trusted? From the moment I committed to keeping my secret and to forgetting it, I'd lost my youth, and that was long before I portrayed an aged woman beneath the stage lights in the Mercury High School auditorium. Youth was so fleeting, indeed.

———

On opening night of *Guys and Dolls*, Pete—who had been cast as one of Nathan Detroit's henchmen—pulled me aside about an hour before the overture was slated to begin. By then, his relationship with Nora had run its course.

"Hey," he said. "I have an idea for our scene."

Near the end of the play, Pete and I had a quick moment together in front of the curtain, designed to keep the crowd entertained while the stage crew reworked the set behind the drapes. After committing some kind of shenanigans outside the mission, my character—cane and all—chased Pete across the stage.

The two of us stood in the hallway, just to the side of the backstage area. He wore a herringbone cap and a thick coat of blush and I had my worn, knotted cane in hand. A friend's grandmother had agreed to loan it to me for the performance.

"What's your idea?" I asked.

"You should hit me with the cane," he said. "It'll be hilarious."

"Aren't you afraid it'll hurt?"

He shook his head. "Nah. The audience will eat it up. Trust me."

Later that night during our scene together, I hiked up my skirt and swatted Pete's back with my cane as we ran across the stage. The onlookers erupted in laughter. When we reached the other side of the stage, the two of us stood in the dark for a moment.

"Come on," he whispered. "You can do better than that. Really *hit* me next time."

During the next performance, I whacked him so hard that the cane split. After we rushed offstage, I put my hand on Pete's back.

"Pete!" I said, breathless. "Are you okay?"

"Are you kidding?" he said. "They loved it!" He paused, touching the welt the cane had left. "Just next time, maybe don't hit me so hard."

By the time we got to the Sunday matinee performance, we'd struck our rhythm and my lopsided gait had turned into a waltz—two beats for my feet, and one for my cane. Thank God for Pete, who still had the power to make me feel young.

———

About two days before Christmas, I sat in the living room of our house, watching the snow come down outside. The year was coming to a close, the wash of white shielding all the dead leaves that hadn't been swept and burned in the fall. When I returned to school in a week and a half, it would be 1998. Slowly, we were inching toward the millennium. Next year at this time, my plans for escape would be in motion. But for now, I waited.

I wasn't far from the phone when it rang. I already had my hand on the receiver when an unexpected number appeared on the caller ID. A trill rang through the house. If I didn't answer, I knew he'd never leave a message. After months of silence, Simon was on the other end of the line. My brain told me he was home for break and he was bored. My gut told me to just pick up the phone already, so I did.

"Hello?" I said.

"Amy," Simon said. "How are you?"

"Fine," I said, hesitant. "How are you?"

"I'm okay."

There was no playful banter, no sense of his usual prescript. Simon was just being Simon, and he sounded tired.

"I need to go shopping for some Christmas gifts. Would you like to come?" He paused. "I'd really like to see you."

When Simon picked me up later that evening, he wasn't driving the jeep. Instead, he pulled up in a white sports car that sat low to the ground.

"What happened to the jeep?" I asked as I climbed into the passenger seat.

"Retired," he said. He smiled from behind the wheel, his hand on the stick shift. We kept our distance. It burned, the way I had him, and the way I didn't.

"You look good," he said.

"Thanks," I answered. "You, too."

We rode about fifteen minutes outside of town to the stretch of wetland that recently had been developed into a huge outdoor outlet mall. It had caused a huge controversy during construction, resulting in patches of untouched marshes dotted throughout the mall's landscape. This mall was the most exciting thing to happen to our area since the Mercury Raceway had come to town. Every Saturday night in summer, the "races," as they were called, packed a stadium at the base of the hill on North Street. Our back-country area was finally becoming known for something else besides summer noise pollution and automobile exhaust.

As we traveled the winding back roads that led to the mall, the silence had no wind to couch it. Night had fallen, and we could see little except the glowing beacon of retail ahead, guiding us toward it. When we arrived, we sat in the car as the engine idled. All summer, Simon took good care to ensure we remained out of the small, though scrutinizing public eye. Now, we were about to enter the most crowded place for miles at the height of its busiest season.

"Well," he said, popping open his door. "Shall we?"

The outlet mall was a gridded maze easy to get lost in, and we did. Simon and I strolled up and down the aisles as Christmas music piped through the outdoor stereo system. The place glowed, every store display decorated with holly and wreaths.

"You could get your mom a sweater," I suggested when we turned the corner at the mall's center. In front of us, a thin wooden bridge suspended over a shallow bit of wetland, now covered in snow. "Or a scarf."

Simon nodded, though I could tell he hadn't heard me.

"Are you all right?" I asked.

In the midst of a crowded square, Simon stopped walking. "I've been miserable," he said.

His honesty surprised me. "Why?" I asked.

"I miss you," he said, looking at me.

"You do?" I spoke softly in a mass of shoppers who yelled and laughed together. They barely noticed the two of us, each of our frozen glances caught up in the other's as the blond wooden bridge behind us became slick with ice.

"I thought about you every day," he said. "And it's been killing me."

Though my hands quivered because of the dropping temperature, I grew hot beneath my jacket. Stripped of his usual flattering quips, Simon bewitched me.

"What do you want?" I asked him.

He lifted his shoulders as an act of surrender. "I just want to be with you."

He didn't touch me or try to kiss me. He didn't try to flatter me as a way to clothe himself. That night at the beach the previous summer, he'd seen me naked when I appeared with my glasses. Now, he was bare before me, revealing himself without the act he hid behind.

I couldn't help but see myself when I looked at Simon—someone who wanted to leave home, and yet couldn't bear to part with it. I forgot all the plans I had to make him pay for the hurt he'd caused. I missed my mirror, even as it tricked me. With Simon, there was no looking backward or forward. There was only now.

Between Christmas and New Year's, Simon and I were inseparable. He had dinner with my family, he took me to my favorite restaurant and ordered me fried ice cream, and we went to the movies. *Titanic* had just come out, and Simon couldn't wait to see it. When we arrived, the theater was packed, and we were lucky to find two adjacent seats in the back. The movie had the kind of storyline Simon always fell for, a romance doomed from the beginning. We both knew how it would end, and still we leaned forward in our seats.

When we exited the theater after the movie ended, I crossed my arms and leaned into the wind. Simon put his arm around my shoulder, and I let him comfort me. The nudity in the movie embarrassed me, but not because Simon was there. It was because Kate Winslet was at ease in her naked skin, a sensation I feared would always be foreign to me. I never felt beautiful; when I looked at myself, all I saw was a lie.

"Sorry there was nudity," Simon said, as if reading my thoughts. "I didn't know."

"Oh, it's okay," I lied, again and again.

Simon knew I'd never have sex with him, and he'd never ask me to. After he confessed how much he hated Mr. Lotte when we drove by the jail over the summer, I knew what happened to his sister Aria still affected his present actions. Though Mr. Lotte and his scandal buried so long ago had brought out the worst in some, it also revealed the best in others.

"I cried like a baby at the end of that movie," Simon said as we climbed into the car and shivered, waiting for the heat to come on. "And I don't even care."

There it was again—that carefree honesty, the kind I thought I needed to squeeze from him in order to stay alive. I was still as rigid as I'd been on all those Saturday mornings before ballet class, and I'd surrendered the one spark that could melt what had frozen. I couldn't continue to warm myself at Simon's fire. I needed to build my own.

By the time New Year's Eve arrived, a pall had been cast over the year's end. The following week, I'd go back to school, and so would Simon. The rush I felt before Christmas had twisted into dread. January could never be as romantic as December. We hadn't talked about what would happen once he left again, but the conversation loomed.

I decided to have a small party in my basement, and the mood was sour. A few of my other friends who were dating college boys found themselves in a similar dilemma. Nobody wanted to be alone on New Year's.

By about ten o'clock, each couple had taken their corners. The basement lights were bright. Simon sat beside me on the couch, brooding.

"I can't make any promises," he said flatly.

I clenched my jaw. "You were the one who called me, remember?"

"I know," he said. "But this is so hard."

"Listen," I said. "I want you to do one thing for me."

"What?"

"E-mail me once a day," I said. "Something short. Send a blank screen. I don't care. Just so I know you thought of me at least once."

He frowned. I was reining him in, and I knew he'd hate it. But I had made a decision. I would be an understudy no longer. I was ready for the lead.

"I can't make any promises," he repeated. "But I'll try."

When the clock struck midnight, we shared a lackluster kiss. We looked at each other, and I knew the spell had been broken.

After Simon returned to college, I welcomed my old routine, studying and preparing to audition for the junior class play. For five days, Simon sent his dutiful e-mail, short, innocuous accounts of his life away from home. Food in the cafeteria, trips to the library, antics with his soccer teammates. It didn't feel as good to tame him as I hoped it might. When Saturday came, by afternoon I hadn't heard from him. By late evening, I still hadn't heard from him. On Sunday morning, I checked my e-mail and found an empty inbox.

The truth: I wanted him to forget. Sitting down in front of the computer, I crafted an e-mail. There was no greeting, no ending, just three sentences:

"I didn't hear from you yesterday, so that means one of two things happened. Either you forgot to e-mail me, or you're dead. For your sake, I hope you're dead."

He responded by Monday, full of excuses. But the curtain had been drawn, and I didn't want another encore.

———

I warded off the chill of being alone by cloaking myself in spotlights and mirrors. A few weeks after Christmas break ended, I was cast as another old woman in the junior class production of *Steel Magnolias*. On opening night, I used the same silver hairspray as I had for *Guys and Dolls*, the same thick, black eyeliner pen to age myself. During the play's run, a woman from town who had volunteered to help backstage took my long, brown hair in her hands and pulled it into a bun behind my head. She brushed and pinned, brushed and pinned. I watched her watch me in the mirror. When she asked me what size dress I wore, it took me a minute to answer.

"A three or four, I think," I said as the brush tore through my hair. "I don't have a lot of dresses."

"A three or four?" She huffed, tying an elastic band around the ponytail she'd made. "That can't be true."

"Why?" I asked.

"Because that's the size I was in high school." She wound my ponytail around and around, creating a bun. "And I was much thinner than you are."

Becca, who had been cast in Dolly Parton's role, came and sat beside me. In the dressing room mirror before us, we looked at each other. Her makeup had been done up—thick, black lashes, glossy red lips. A bouffant only fitting for a southern beauty shop owner. Together, we watched the woman in the mirror, dressed in an old sweatshirt and jeans, a fray of bobby pins in her mouth. Only after sticking in the final pin did she look up and stare back at the source of our reflections, a mirror that had become a glass dagger in the eyes of the envious.

As it was known to do, winter overstayed its welcome and hung around deep into March. The colder months were especially hard on the town's elderly, and one frigid Sunday evening, Pure Heart Presbyterian asked the teenagers in the congregation to pay visits to those unable to leave their homes. "Shut-ins," they were called. We met up in the church parking lot about six in the evening, just around the time most of the townsfolk would be closing themselves in for the night. Two by two, we paired up and got an address. No directions needed; there wasn't a street or a face in this town we hadn't seen a million times. Our town had fewer people in it than passengers aboard a large luxury cruise liner.

Aaron and I paired up, and I offered to drive. We'd both gotten our licenses earlier that year, but Aaron was still saving all of his tips from working nights and weekends at Coyote's Pizza so he could buy himself a car. When my sister got her license a few years before, my parents purchased a car for their children to use, since all three of us were so close in age. With my sister away at college and my brother a year from turning sixteen, I had become the primary driver. When Aaron climbed into the seat, he fiddled with the knob on the side and the seat glided back, creating enough room for his long legs.

I hadn't told Aaron or any of the other church boys about how I'd backslid with Simon over Christmas break. I'd failed myself by trusting Simon again, and I'd failed my faithful church boys, too. When he'd broken up with me in the fall, the church boys crowded around me like a soft, boyish blanket. "He's a dick," one of them said. Though Aaron had seen the end from the beginning and warned me, he never chastised me or said, "I told you so." Even if he knew what had happened, he'd never say a word.

We went to visit a woman who lived alone at the end of a long, winding driveway not too far from where Aaron worked at Coyote's on Ashville Road. The house was built far into a shallow hill, and as I turned down the driveway, we had to tilt our heads up to see the candles shining in the windows.

At the front door, we waited after ringing the doorbell. I could feel my entire body contracting in the cold. Inside the house, we heard a soft creaking as the shut-in made her way to the window. We saw her soft features in the candlelight as she peered out at us. Smiling, she pulled open the door wide and waved us indoors, as if to say, *Come in, come in, before you catch your death.*

Once inside her living room, we shed our layers quickly as the furnace blasted heat from the corner. I'd soon forget her name, but I'd remember the chiming clock, the floral wallpaper, the matching doilies on the couch and arm chair. She said she was "from Mercury, born and raised." We entered, we sat. She served us water on a silver tray. The clock chimed. The wind blew. Someone's stomach growled.

"Look at the two of you," she said to us from her rocking chair. "So young."

Sitting across from her on a velvet couch, I wondered if we were staring into our future. Born in Mercury, lived in Mercury, died in Mercury. She must have thought she was staring into her past.

Often, the young and the old in Mercury looked at each other from either side of impenetrable glass. We—the young—wanted to get out, and they wanted to get back. *Tock tock tock tock.* I couldn't help but wonder when the switch occurred, when someone went from what *is* to what *was*, like all those town fires. Was it high school graduation, the clock striking at midnight, and all the Cinderellas returned to their rags and soot?

Aaron sat on the couch and didn't say much. He was never one to offer comfort, though I found his presence very comforting. Accustomed to emptiness, he never felt the need to fill the air with words. So the three of us just sat, drank tepid tap water, and stared at the moon.

Without any older boys to interfere, by summertime Aaron and I had become a close, platonic pair. He knew me like no one else. His voice could shoot through the fences I hid behind, and on the day we dove into the heart of a cave in West Virginia, it did.

Each summer, Pure Heart Presbyterian took a weeklong camping trip to West Virginia to serve the local poor and experience the mountains.

On a stifling Wednesday afternoon, thirty of us packed into the vans and spent forty-five minutes winding around Appalachian roads, headed for a spot to go cave diving.

When we reached our destination, the trail of vans pulled over onto the side of the road. I looked out the window and couldn't detect a cave opening. Instead, I saw a steep, green hill smothered with trees. When we all got out of the van, I realized this was no mistake. Somewhere in the mess of pine was the entrance to our cave. Tucking my flashlight between my skin and the band of my Levi's, I started to climb.

The cave's dark opening was tall and slender, the shape of a screaming mouth. Forming a single line, we entered it. I waited near the end of the group to watch girls with bandanas and boys with headlamps disappear into the dark. I hovered, turning on my flashlight and aiming its dim light into the opening. I saw nothing.

"Can't we get lost in there?" I asked Aaron, who stood behind me in line.

"You'll be fine," he said.

Aaron wasn't afraid. He wasn't excited, either. He strolled ahead as I hung back until everyone entered but the experienced cavers bringing up the rear. Reluctantly, I fell in line.

Once I entered the cave, daylight shut off like a light bulb. As we climbed deeper into its throat, my teeth chattered and I slipped on the gritty sludge covering the ground. I lost track of time as the path got harder and harder to maneuver and the tunnels narrowed. The talking died down, and just the squeak of rubber soles on wet rocks echoed through the cavity.

We came to a spot with a wide gap between two rocks, and we had to jump across it to keep moving forward—or upward—or downward. I couldn't orient myself. Two older boys crammed themselves into slivers between the boulders to help each of us across. When my turn came, one of them grabbed my arm. I resisted.

"I don't want to." I had an acute distaste for enclosed spaces like this one. Situations without an easy exit made me panic. I couldn't remember it then, but Mr. Lotte's basement felt a lot like a dark cave, with the piano and his body barring me from the closed door. The church boys craved the rush of fear that activities like this created, but the fear felt too real to me. I didn't want anyone or anything blocking my escape.

"You gonna sit here in the dark, then?" one of the boys said. "You better hope we come back the same way."

I pointed my flashlight into the crevice and saw nothing. No bottom, no sides, just black. I had no choice. I had to grasp his hand and lunge. Once I wedged a foot in between the crags of two rocks, they pulled my body across the gap.

Finally we reached our destination—a tomblike, shallow clearing. Everyone ducked as we crowded inside it. Some leaned against the wall, others crouched on their knees. I knelt rigidly, shivering and clutching my flashlight. It felt like I was breathing with a bag over my head.

The guide moved to the center of the group. "All right, everybody," he said. "Flashlights off."

One by one, the lights went out. A scorching imprint remained on my eyelids, but soon it dissipated. We waited. Throats cleared. We heard a dull dripping sound.

"This," the guide said with a pause, "is what hell is like."

I restrained my own urge to grab the person I couldn't see sitting next to me. The air around me was the color of coke, the dark powder coal becomes after it burns.

I tried to hold my breath, but couldn't. Somewhere to the left of me, I heard the smack-smacking of two kids making out. The air smelled like must. I started to wonder if this was where I'd die, squeezed into a hairline crack in the side of the earth.

I have to get out of here, I kept thinking.

I started to recite things in my head. *One, two, three, four ... For all have sinned and fall short of the glory of God. Romans 3:23.*

This is what hell is like.

Our father, who art in heaven, hallowed be thy name.

This is what hell is like.

Forgive us our debts, as we forgive our debtors.

Thisiswhathellislike.

Lead us not into temptation, but deliver us from evil.

This. Is. What. Hell. Is. Like.

Water spilled from my eyes, and I squeezed them shut. I felt the breath of an invisible moment on my neck, the specter of a man sitting on a piano bench in a brown basement, and I shivered. *Don't you cry*, I told myself. *Don't you be a pussy.* But then my eyes turned to waterfalls. I hid my face in my sweatshirt.

"Okay, everybody," the guide finally said. "Lights on."

I heard blessed murmurs, cracking knees, the click of my own thumb. I looked into the soft tunnel-glow of my flashlight and found Aaron at the end of it, staring back at me. I diverted my eyes and moved to the front of the line, hoping he hadn't seen.

Later that night at the campground, I sat next to Aaron around the campfire while he played his guitar. The group was small; most had gone to bed after tiring themselves out in the cave. Aaron never went to bed early. He'd stay at the campfire until it went out, and the next morning he'd be up, the first person out of his tent to stoke it.

Beside me, Aaron turned the knobs of his guitar and tinkered with the strings. I watched them vibrate as he strummed and pressed them.

"You were scared in that cave, weren't you?" he said. A soft melody formed beneath his fingers.

"So what?"

"So nothing." He smiled.

He ran his thumb against the guitar strings and began to sing a hymn.

"You can't sing," I said. Aaron shrugged. "Neither can Bob Dylan."

He started the second verse and I closed my eyes. I wanted to breathe in the smoke. I always felt closest to God in places like this, sitting by a campfire and a friend who loved me, no matter my sins.

"Hey," Aaron said. "You were in my dream last night."

"I was? What happened?"

"Can't remember."

"What did I look like?" I asked.

He tilted his head, and I saw the red sunburn on the back of his neck. "What do you mean?"

"I mean, did I look sweaty and dirty like this, or did I look normal?"

"That's a stupid question." He looked at me without blinking. "You were you."

He looked back at the fire and tucked his guitar pick beneath the strings. Above us, the sky opened up to an unfenced pasture of stars.

So simple, his words. *You were you*, he'd said. I was I. So long ago, when I'd stood on the cliff of that diving board, wondering if I'd had it in me to jump, my father had asked me a question. *Is fear going to rule you?* Again and again, I had to remind myself of my answer. *No.* I didn't let fear rule me then, and I wouldn't let it rule me now.

I didn't need a man to mirror. I didn't need Simon. I'd sat in that dark cave, the closest estimation of hell, and it hadn't killed me.

Yes. I was I, and I was getting out.

♪

Just like the fires in our small town, in memory the past gets rewritten. When friends of the defendant take the stand on his behalf, they urge the judge to see the Howard Lotte that they know and love, a man who is more saint than sinner. "I truly can say that I know of no good man that better exemplifies my view of what a good and decent man should be," one of his fellow teachers says. "I can honestly say that he was one of the most caring mainstream teachers I have ever worked with," says another. *Truly, honestly, madly, deeply*—we would have sworn such girlish words were used by one of us in the throes of infatuation (girls are so prone to exaggeration, so they say—isn't that what brought this trouble on in the first place?) rather than a late morning courtroom, if we hadn't seen the transcript for ourselves. Seven witnesses, including Lotte himself, all use different words to ask for the same thing:

Please, please, Your Honor. Don't send him to jail.

No matter what the judge decides, half of Mercury will be outraged. The sentence will be too harsh, or not harsh enough, and each side will blame the other for sending our town to the shitter. *This used to be a good and decent place to live*, they'll say. *Now look at us.* At the hearing, the judge is determined to set the record straight—not on Lotte's behalf, but for the town itself.

THE COURT: Are you a victim of perceived impropriety?

THE DEFENDANT: No.

THE COURT: Are you a victim of parental hysteria?

THE DEFENDANT: No, sir.

THE COURT: A letter dated August 6, 1992: "We believe the charges brought against him are false and were prefabricated by the students involved." What would you say to those people?

THE DEFENDANT: It's not true.

THE COURT: Letter dated August 6, 1992: "My prayer is that his guilty plea is not the result of poor attorney advice." Is your plea the result of poor attorney advice?

THE DEFENDANT: No, it's not, Your Honor.

THE COURT: Is it a result of the fact that you are guilty?

THE DEFENDANT: Yes, Your Honor.

THE COURT: Letter dated August 12, 1992: "I believe that all the charges of corruption of morals of minors and indecent assault to be the result of a conspiracy." Is that correct?

THE DEFENDANT: There is no conspiracy in this community.

THE COURT: So, Mr. Lotte, no fellow teacher, no friend, no associate, no former student, no member of this community should proceed on the belief that you are innocent in any way of these charges; is that correct?

THE DEFENDANT: That is correct.

Finally, the judge grants the parents a small victory, assuring the courtroom he will not be swayed by Mr. Lotte's good deeds: "So the fact that you are very good and have done very good things in your community is neutral. It fits in with the profile."

"This is a great tragedy for everyone," the judge goes on to say. "But there's only one person who perpetrated the tragedy; it is you, Mr. Lotte."

After his sentencing, Mr. Lotte serves one year, one month, and eight days. *I always knew he wasn't quite right*, some will say. No one will admit to being duped by the great and powerful Lotte, and many still won't admit his guilt. An unspoken treaty seeps into our town, from the city limits by the McDonald's to the flooded strip mines just outside of town where kids sneak off to swim: *Never speak of this again.*

At the beginning, this truce seems easier to achieve than "forgive and forget," and for the most part, it is. If there are two things people in Mercury aren't good at, it's forgiving and forgetting. We trade in grudges and well-worn memories; they fill in the space between Friday night football games and Sunday morning services. But as silence winds itself around lampposts and mailboxes, school desks and overturned basketball hoops, the words masquerading as a peace offering—*Never speak of this again*—reveal themselves to be a communal spell. No one in Mercury can find the words to speak about Mr. Lotte even if we want to, and nobody does.

And what about us good girls? We've done our fair share in restitching the tapestry of our town. Distanced as we are from the drama, we can't deny that our silence has rendered us accomplices. The prisoner's dilemma is at it again—we didn't rat out Mr. Lotte, and he reciprocated in kind. The old Mercury saying is turning out to be true: you're only as good as the company you keep. Over time, our memories start to resemble a dead fire the morning after it burned bright. The matter of memory still exists, but we can't even hope to reconstruct it from the cinder it has become.

PART III

All the Prettiest Girls

Impostor

MERCURY WAS A TOWN where repetition masked itself as tradition. Every hour on the hour, the courthouse clock in the center of town chimed. Every morning, a group of retired men known around Mercury as "the Romeos" dined on eggs and bacon at the local diner. Each February, Emmett the Elf appeared at the winter craft fair with rouged cheeks and jingling shoes. He always brought his flute and his bad attitude. And who could forget the she-minstrel at the artisan fest held on the courthouse lawn each summer? Every July, she wore a skirt made of men's neckties and sang folk songs while sashaying around the yard. You could count on these people like the chiming of the clock.

And each year in September, every blue-collar girl at Mercury High School who ever dreamed of becoming a princess finally got her shot. Like this: on the second day of the school year, the senior class gathered to cast ballots for the annual homecoming court. Six lucky boys and girls were chosen by their peers to become Appalachian royalty—the perennial sparks that flashed against our monochromatic backdrop. After five weeks of fame, the entire school would vote for one boy and one girl to rise above the rest and receive their reward: a sash, a crown, and a wildest dream come true.

Homecoming queen. Just the sound of it made all the girls fawn.

Don't be fooled. Homecoming didn't exist to welcome alumni back to their old haunts. Instead, it snapped a still-life of the town's latest crop of kids before they ascended into legends (*Remember Bobby? He could nail a three-pointer from midcourt*) or descended into has-beens (*That Cassie could have done something with her life if she'd never gotten herself pregnant*). The significance was larger than tradition or title. For the girl on top, it was a destination. For everyone else, it became the jewel of envy—the private allure of fantasy and the menacing grip of the impossible.

Homecoming in Mercury was a small-town album destined to repeat itself. Mothers in town had graced the court when they were students at Mercury High School, and the school kept pictures to prove it. Always a well-cut crew, the court consumed multipage spreads in every yearbook. Leafing through them in the library, you'd see them—every year, a new batch of girls. Glance at the photographs, and you'd see a string of paper dolls. Focus, and you'd discover the clenched muscles behind their smiles. Linger, and you'd see a group of girls taking what they thought they could get.

My own mother had never been on any "court" since she grew up in a town even smaller than Mercury where, for a time, she only went to school four days a week. At age eighteen, while Mercury girls were primping and parading at homecoming, my mother was fashioning her plans for escape just like I was. Her cello, her ticket out, gave her a scholarship that brought her to western Pennsylvania. For the twenty-five years she'd lived here, she hated the homecoming charade. "If I were in charge," she said, "I'd cancel the whole thing."

Fat chance. Canceling homecoming would be as un-American as canceling Christmas. None of us was immune to its power. Even my father had been named to the court back in 1973. I'd seen him in his yearbook, where he was remembered as a star wrestler and a football player. His hair was blondish-brown, hanging just below his ears. The yearly rite of homecoming had become impenetrable and mythic, sired long before my parents' generation, and would survive long after I was dead.

During early fall of my senior year, my familiar weakness remained closer to me than any confidante. I didn't *want* to want to be chosen, and yet I wanted it still. Getting voted by my peers promised to be both the reward and the antidote for the choice I'd made so long ago to fall in line and stay silent. A validation of my lie and a remedy for the guilt. The paradox spun me around more times than I could count.

On the second day of school, I joined my classmates as we clamored toward the cafeteria. About a hundred of us spread out among the tables; no one sat side by side. These were answers we wouldn't dare reveal. It was time to do what all the classes before us had done, and all the classes after us would continue after we disappeared.

I stared at my empty bubble sheet, looking back and forth between it and the corresponding list of senior boys' and girls' names. Carefully, I chose the names of six boys, most of them from church. Then I moved on to the girls.

I was no stranger to popularity contests. They were a cinder block in the architecture of small-town life. Even local churches felt it necessary to rank their children. My first spar for supremacy occurred during Vacation Bible School in a neighboring town when I was only eight years old. The theme that year revolved around friendship, and at the end of the week a "best friend" was selected from every class by vote. The unintended lesson: Friendship was not laying down your life for someone else. Friendship was sizing up your competition.

Our class of girls was small, no more than five, and three of the students abstained from voting.

"This is stupid," a girl named Mary said. "Why can't we all be best friends?"

That left two votes still in play—Carly's and mine. We each wrote a name, folded our papers, and handed them to our teacher. We watched as she opened them. She smiled as she shook her head. "So sweet," she whispered to the other teacher. "Carly and Amy chose each other."

I realized then that naiveté had the power to claim women as well as girls. The teacher thought we'd voted for each other, but we hadn't. We'd each chosen ourselves.

"Looks like we'll have to have a tiebreaker," the teacher said. "I'll go around and ask some of the other teachers for input."

I wanted to object, knowing that many of the other teachers were Carly's relatives and therefore biased. But if I called attention to it, the teacher would realize that I'd voted for myself, so I remained quiet—something I was too good at, even then. During the final ceremony, the crowd clapped as Carly accepted the trophy.

In the cafeteria as I rushed to make a decision, Carly's young face flashed in my mind. Once a perfect archetype for the sickly myth of the good girl, she would have been a shoo-in for the court, had she been able to stay in Mercury. Had she never been accused of lying about Mr. Lotte.

Where was Carly now? Some other town, some other high school, where no one knew her past and no one knew the friend who hadn't stood beside her. Though I'd banished Mr. Lotte from memory, Carly remained there, just beneath the surface and beyond my reach. My ghostly obverse, Carly had chosen what I could not; she'd paid prices I would not.

"One more minute," the proctor said. Other students rose from their seats and headed for the door. Noise and murmurs slowly returned.

You can't vote for someone who isn't there, I told myself. But as I filled in the circle corresponding to my name, I couldn't help feeling that the spot rightfully belonged to someone else. Once upon a time, Carly and I had both wanted to woo the heart of Mercury. The difference between us: she hadn't bowed to it, and I had fallen to my knees.

The following day during ninth period, we all knew it was coming. *The announcement.* I waited in German class with Aaron, who couldn't be bothered with popularity contests. When the loudspeaker crackled, the room silenced.

"May I have your attention, please, for a special announcement," someone said into a microphone. "The members of this year's homecoming court are . . ."

Every classroom door and window hung wide open. No one in the whole school made a sound. It felt just like that early afternoon so long ago when the car dealership near Mercury's elementary school had its explosion, and Principal Mellon's voice echoed on the intercom. It was right at the height of the Lotte scandal, not a month before he'd officially plead guilty to his crimes. We knew, then—even before Principal Mellon spoke—that something great or terrible, or something great *and* terrible—had occurred. The line between awe and horror was so fine we often had to straddle it.

But today was a day of great and terrible things in the Land of Mercury. In less than a minute, my name was called, and I turned into one of the lucky ones.

This year, *seven* boys and *seven* girls had been chosen instead of six. There must have been a tie. When the list concluded, the school awoke from its stupor. "Seven?" students whispered. "Did they list *seven*?"

Frau Zimmer offered me congratulations.

"*Viel Glück*," she said.

"*Danke*, Frau Zimmer," I answered. The local fame I'd chased throughout my youth felt more like nakedness as the unchosen lifted their gazes from their desks and examined me. Now a member of Mercury's most elite and long-standing clique, I'd been dubbed a girl who was "interesting to watch."

How many girls? Seven girls. Seven girls came forward, seven were separated from the crowd. Seven girls for Lotte, seven girls for now, and an entire town turned its eye.

Even as I dove deep into the throes of homecoming, I still fought for a life raft. I knew I couldn't remain one of the seven girls for that very reason—I was one of seven, a stand-in among a fan of paper dolls. That's what a good girl was: one who folded in on herself. I needed to be real, sins and all, and I'd finally found my escape route.

Last summer while school was out, I'd fallen in love with a staircase. Near the end of July, my parents and I took the six-hour trip to Ithaca, a hippie town in upstate New York, to see my first and only Ivy

League university. We did it on our own; the guidance department at my school existed only to funnel students to local colleges. Pushing past the borders they'd set was not only arrogant; it was a betrayal of the worst kind.

But Cornell was a place like no other. I saw for the first time the kind of access that stature can provide. In the center of its sprawling campus stood a tall, lean clock tower and, next to it, a library. This university, we soon discovered, had libraries *inside* its libraries. When I walked through the Andrew Dickson White Library, I fell for it harder and faster than for any boy in Mercury. The room looked just like the set of *My Fair Lady*. A bright red carpet stretched across the floor, leather couches with deep cushions and fancy buttons accentuated the bright windows, and marble heads perched on pillars. But the *shelves*. Three floors of wrought iron stacks rose before me, each flanked with a spiral staircase. I imagined myself climbing a ladder to the top row like Professor Henry Higgins, sliding from left to right in search of the perfect book. There were thirty thousand to choose from, and this was just one of Cornell's twenty libraries. The stairwell, thin and dark, spiraled upward in a cloud of hardcover books, twirling like the hem of a dancing woman's skirt.

The odds were against me. When my parents and I met with an admissions officer, he frowned. The balding man with a mustache like a piece of white chalk remained stoic as I listed my accolades. Senior class treasurer, school newspaper editor, president of the chorus, president of the speech and debate team. I did my best to look him straight in the eye, as all good-girls-going-places should.

"How are your grades?" he asked.

"Good," I answered. "Straight A's."

"Class rank?"

"Number two."

He raised his eyebrows as if I'd finally impressed him. "How big is your graduating class?"

"One-twenty-five."

He let out a mild snort. "You need to find yourself a bigger senior class."

He laughed, but he wasn't joking. I needed a miracle. But I'd always known I was the Queen of the Longshots.

Despite my intentions to get out of Mercury, my own affection for artifice threatened to turn my quest to become real into a fantasy. In the midst of the school's homecoming preparations, I auditioned for the role I'd been waiting for. For so long I'd imagined playing the part of Rosie in *Bye Bye Birdie*, though I wasn't fit for it. Rosie had dark skin and hair, while my skin was fair and my hair had golden highlights; she was a headstrong career woman, and I still looked barely sixteen. Even so, I had all her songs memorized, and I sang one for my audition.

When I stepped into the music room to perform for the panel of judges, I was a different girl than the one who had auditioned for *Anything Goes* three years earlier. That girl had faltered on her high notes, stuck her hands in her pockets, and said she'd take any role available. This time, I strode in with polite confidence. This was my only shot, and I knew it.

The one person who might have been more suited for Rosie's role than me was the one person no longer around to claim it. Even at age ten, Carly had been an angelic vocalist. Though she'd been gone for almost seven years, at times I still found myself filling her shoes. But I didn't let myself dwell on it. It would only ruin my chances to get what I thought I'd always wanted—a prime opportunity to act like someone else for all of Mercury to see.

Even before she left town, Carly and I had been too alike not to resist each other. We fought over any opportunity to put ourselves on display. I had already fallen into Carly's shadow during our kindergarten play—I was in the chorus of chicks and she was the miller's wife—

and when our second-grade class performed *The Real Princess*, I was determined not to let it happen again. I feared my future: some of us were destined to be millers' wives, and some of us to be chicks.

Our teacher, Mrs. Palmer, cast me in the role of the queen. The plot was what one might expect: the king and queen were on a hunt to find the perfect princess for their son to marry. Young, enterprising ladies came from near and far to audition for them, but the king and queen snuffed out the fakes. "She was not a real princess," they said. At the play's climax, the real princess appeared. When the queen placed a pea underneath a pile of mattresses, the real princess tossed and turned all night while all the other counterfeit princesses slept like rocks. Once her authenticity was verified, the princess married the prince, and the two lived happily ever after. A "real" princess—the phrase was an illusion in itself.

Who else but Carly could be the perfect choice to play the beautiful, youthful princess? I nursed my wounds by telling myself my role was equally important. "You have the most lines in the whole play," Mrs. Palmer told me when I asked her why Carly had gotten the princess role. "And the first line, too."

On the day of the performance, our classroom was transformed into a stage with a seating area in front of it. Mrs. Palmer constructed a backstage area by hanging a large piece of felt from a rope slung from one wall to the other by the bathroom. Minutes before the production was about to begin, Carly and I started to fight.

I stood with my hands on my hips, wearing a royal blue gown I'd gotten for being a flower girl the year before. "You might be the princess," I said to Carly. "But I'm the star of the play."

She batted her eyelashes. "I'm the star. The play is named after me."

"No," I countered. "*I'm* the star."

Carly's tone matched mine. "I. AM."

"No, I AM!"

Realizing we'd reached a stalemate, we called in Mrs. Palmer to settle the dispute.

"Which one of us is the star of the play?" I asked. "Which one?"

Mrs. Palmer smiled and placed a light hand on each of our backs. "Everyone here is the star because without everyone, we couldn't put on the play."

In the backstage of all my performances, naiveté and cunning seemed to come hand-in-hand. I told myself that Mrs. Palmer didn't want to injure Carly's fragile feelings. I didn't stop to consider she might not want to hurt mine.

The morning after the *Bye Bye Birdie* tryouts, I went to the main office window to inspect the cast list. Rosie's name was listed first. It was the role I was meant to play, personal appearance be damned, and I finally got it.

It was a dirty business, getting everything I wanted. As homecoming hysteria ballooned, facsimiles of my face started to appear everywhere. The photographs from the annual homecoming photo shoot ran in all the local newspapers and were displayed behind a glass case in the main hall of the school right next to the gymnasium. Every day that fall, I beheld evidence of what I thought I'd always desired—my name listed in the annals of Mercury's proud history. The first time I'd seen pictures like this, I was just a seventh grader still finding my way around a new school. The main hallway was always flush with people pushing and shoving to get to class on time. That fall, the court's homecoming pictures graced the glass display case just as they would five years later.

At thirteen, I'd felt giddy when I saw the collection of all my idols in one picture. I couldn't wait for the homecoming game. It would be my first time witnessing a new crowning. Though I wouldn't get to vote until I was in ninth grade, I wanted Roxanna Ryan to win. She represented everything I hoped to be by the time I turned seventeen— tall, slender, beautiful, and captain of the dance line with the white pom-poms to prove it. When I looked at myself in the mirror, it was Roxanna Ryan that I wanted to see.

As there was every year, a lot of buzz surrounded the projections about who would win—Roxanna, or one of the other hopefuls. One girl on the court named Dana had been dating the same boy since seventh grade, and rumor suggested if she was crowned queen at the football game, Kurt was going to propose right there on the fifty-yard line. Some insisted it was just a propaganda tactic to steal votes away from Rachel Hart, the favorite to win. A Barbie-like girl with bleached blond hair, Rachel had bangs that spiked like an ocean wave. You could crunch her curls in your fist because of all the hairspray. The week before voting, Rachel skulked the lunch tables of swing voters, offering to take up their lunch trays. Her tactic worked, and that Friday night Rachel was crowned Mercury High School homecoming queen of 1993.

Five years after admiring these beauties for the first time, I walked past my own picture thumbtacked to the wall behind a glass pane. The main hall was crazed with kids waiting out the four minutes that hung between classes. I caught my own likeness in my periphery, but I didn't stop to look at the picture. That picture wasn't me, but what Mercury had fashioned out of me. Behind the glass display was a flat version of myself that everyone—even I—mistook me for. A girl with a soluble spine, a girl who wouldn't cause trouble. A girl who looked like everyone else.

Just before I passed the glass case, I heard someone call my name. I turned and looked behind me, but saw no one.

"Hi, Amy!" The voice chirped again.

I tilted my head down and saw a small seventh-grade girl beaming up at me. I scanned her face, which of course I'd seen before. There were no faces in town I hadn't seen a hundred times. But how did she know my name? I didn't know hers.

"Hi," I said back.

But as I returned her greeting, I saw it wasn't quite me she was admiring. The girl looked just beyond my shoulder at the photograph of me in a black dress I'd never wear again with a pink scarf I didn't tie around my own neck. Next to the photo, someone had taken the time to write my name in bold block letters.

AMY BURNS

So *that* was how she knew me. I'd just become this girl's Roxanna Ryan.

Dressed in denim and diamond studs, this girl just *looked* like someone destined for the court five years from now. When I'd been in seventh grade, I'd been a bookish brunette with glasses and braces. A force, perhaps, no one had seen coming. Around here, people boasted they could predict the future homecoming courts ten years out, like hard winters in a Farmer's Almanac. No one had any money to invest in anything, so townsfolk betted on the youth instead. If I were betting, I would have put my money on this girl in front of me, golden-eyed and giggling. Her blond hair would only improve her chances. Standing beside her, I was no longer myself. I was a surrogate for Roxanna Ryan, and soon, this girl would be a surrogate for me.

Behind me in the hallway, my name shouted itself to passersby.

AMY BURNS

Not just a name, it was also a sentence. Amy burns. Amy burns. Amy burns.

The girl looked slain, as if she'd just spotted a celebrity. And in this town's crooked way, she had. In the glass case, a glimpse of our reflection: her infatuated gaze, my synthetic smile, and the photograph presiding over us like some kind of queenly impostor.

)

Here's a secret from one royal impostor to another: our lies are turning us old. We are aging; we can feel it by the time we return to school in September after Mr. Lotte spends his first few nights in jail. Our faces still resemble baby peaches while our insides curl into tumbleweeds. Those of us entering sixth grade—the grade Mr. Lotte taught every year until now—hope that being the oldest kids in school will make us feel like queens instead of subjects.

We get what we want, as so many pretty girls do, but the sensation inspires more fear than euphoria. Even at eleven and twelve, it's possible to feel old. It wasn't so long ago that we moved from a one-digit age to two, and it doesn't escape us that we might never experience it again. Does anyone live to be a hundred? The paradox of the young ruler is too quixotic to be real, and we soon realize that our youth has abandoned us.

After a few weeks in school, we start to suspect that a sixth-grade teacher named Mr. Westerly feels the same way. He testified at Mr. Lotte's sentence hearing, stating that the two of them were as close as any two men could be. For decades, they have both been teachers, husbands, vets, and friends with each other.

"I was in war!" Mr. Westerly likes to say to his classroom, which some of us are in that year. "What war do you think I was in?"

"World War II?" someone in the back guesses, and Mr. Westerly sighs.

"How old do you think I am?" he asks.

The class looks around and shrugs; no one has any clue to his age, other than his salt-and-pepper hair and his thick glasses with the darkened lenses. But he has always looked this way (as evidenced in both past and future yearbooks), so much so that it appears he isn't aging at all. But we know better than to judge by appearances.

"I fought in the Korean War," Mr. Westerly tells his class after no one can guess correctly. "It's also known as the Forgotten War, because no one remembers it."

These are the moments that Mr. Westerly slips inside himself, and his class knows to stay quiet. Sometimes while his students read silently at their desks, he pens rough drafts of letters to his daughter. We know because we've spied his yellow legal pad over his shoulder, watching him strike through his own words with the same red pen he uses to grade our research essays on white tigers and automobile pistons. The tattoo coiled around his forearm bears the name of a woman who isn't his wife.

"Who is that?" one of us asked him once. "That girl on your arm."

"None of your business," was his answer.

We share an odd kinship with Mr. Westerly, all of us haunted by events no one claims to remember. Does he or any of the other supporters ever visit Mr. Lotte while he serves his time, after all the fighting ceased? No one likes to be reminded of an indiscretion, and worse—no one likes to be seen loitering outside the jail with the wives who wait out in the cold to see their incarcerated husbands during visiting hours. For most of 1993, Mrs. Lotte is one of them, and she looks like she doesn't belong.

She keeps her job at the school, though we don't talk to her anymore because she doesn't really speak to anyone. Her step has lost its spring, and her smile droops. She isn't spotted with the rest of our town at the 1992 homecoming game, or any other homecoming after that, where each year the girls who had once been her husband's piano students take turns prancing around the football field with the hopes of being voted queen of the senior girls.

We pretend to be young rulers with the same vigor we pretend to emerge unscathed from the Lotte scandal. The potency of innocence exists only in our imaginations, and there is no escaping it. Mr. Lotte has stained us all—his students, his friends, his children, his wife. Just like lies and forgotten sacrifices, the truth can turn a person old, too.

Paper Doll

IF HOMECOMING HEAT reached its climax at the Friday night football game, Spirit Week tendered the foreplay. Spanning the five days that led up to the evening of a new queen's coronation, Spirit Week made itself new each day by featuring a different theme chosen by the cheerleading squad. Twin Day. 70s Day. Pajama Day. Blue-and-White Day was reserved for Friday every year; football players wore their jerseys, cheerleaders their uniforms, and someone always offered to paint an "M" on willing cheeks as an ode to our fearless mascot, the Mercury Mustang. These themes complemented the week's holiday festivities, which included—aside from the big game—a parade through town, a bonfire, a pep rally, and the court's pregame jaunt around the football field.

As Spirit Week progressed, the school transformed. The cheerleaders hung banners with the star players' jersey numbers painted on them. The homecoming committee strung streamers in doorways and tinsel and balloons in the long corridor leading to the cafeteria. Excitement infected everyone, even the staff. In the middle of Spirit Week, I paid a visit to the principal in hopes that the excitement had boosted his mood. For the second time, I spent my lunch period trying to coax him to approve my transcripts so I could send in my application to Cornell for early decision.

Everyone in the school knew that the Mercury High School transcripts were a joke. Blotchy, mismatched quilts of information held together by Scotch tape, they were an embarrassment. I'd seen the guidance staff handle them before; they held them at arm's length as if the papers were dirty diapers. I'd even heard that a girl had been rejected by William & Mary because the guidance counselor had left coffee stains on her transcript. Mercury kids, he was known to say, don't go to Ivy League colleges.

I wasn't about to let their apathy cost me the first true thing I'd ever wanted for myself. The week before school started, I'd started to create my own transcripts. With the help of a Mercury mother who had done the same for her daughter, I spent hours on the transcripts before printing them on fine linen paper. The first time I met with the principal, my transcripts were leagues ahead of the school's cryptic, photocopied sheets. I knew it, and he knew it. Still, he scribbled all over them, demanding I change minute details like "German, Level Four" to "German IV" before handing the sheets back to me.

"Okay," I said as I stood up from the seat across from his desk. "I'll be back."

"You do have a backup school in mind, don't you?" he asked before I left. "In case you don't get into Cornell?"

I looked him straight in the eye. "I'll find a backup when I need it."

Now in his office for the second time, he leaned back in his chair and stroked his mustache as he reviewed the material. Just outside his office, blue-and-white streamers hung in the main hallway as cheerleaders continued to paint banners for Friday's big game.

"All right." The principal sighed and sat up. "I'll stamp it."

As if Mercury itself somehow knew how badly I wanted out, Thursday night of Spirit Week was the last town fire I ever took part in. At dusk, the homecoming amoeba prepared to parade through town. Its course had already been set, and it was an expanded version of the path all the students took the day of the explosion at the McCandless car dealership: starting at the elementary school and ending at the high school where a homecoming bonfire waited to be lit.

In the elementary school parking lot, someone handed me a bucket of candy, and I had to pull my hands out from the cuffs of my sweater to hold it. The air was getting colder now. Inside the bucket, I found peppermints, Smarties, and butterscotch in golden cellophane, all the hard candy flavors I used to collect as a child when I'd stood on the side of the road, watching the floats as they passed by and dreaming of the day when I would get my turn.

First up was the band, always the band. I still loved the deep, rhythmic pound of the bass drum and the shallow smack of a drumstick against a snare drum's rim. The sound seeped into my chest and spilled out of it at the same time. It made me think of autumn, of the spark that came from performing for a stadium against the chill of nightfall. My heart burned brightest when the rest of my body had grown cold.

The sun had started to set. After four blows of a whistle, the Mighty Mercury Mustang Marching Machine took off, turning the crisp corner one row at a time. Up next, the class floats fell in line behind the band. A series of gleaming fire engines followed next. The penultimate display featured the MHS football team and cheerleaders clumped together on hay bales that had been tossed onto a flatbed trailer. The boys looked so fresh in their jerseys paired with faded Levis and Wranglers, the girls in their MHS sweaters and turtlenecks. A small homecoming miracle: on this float, there were two boys for every girl.

Last, seven cars with their tops down formed a convertible convoy. When we pulled out of the lot, a crowd had already gathered. Lawn chairs flanked the sidewalk, and children jumped on top of gutters and flailed their arms. "Candy! Candy!" they shouted. Young mothers hung back, cradling babies wrapped in blankets. Fans bordered both sides of the route all the way from the elementary school to the high school. They made a tunnel of people, a preparation fit for hometown royalty.

As we snaked through town, my escort Luke and I tossed candy from the back of the convertible, where we sat enthroned, our dirty boots scuffing the backseat's upholstery. We smiled and waved. I felt my steel heart melting. It hurt, how perfect this moment was. I knew it was real—I could feel the hard candy in my palm, the crisp wind on

my face. I could hear the crowds cheer as we passed and the hypnotiz-
ing thump of the bass drum as we moved.

And yet my constant sacrifice for this ultimate chance to put myself on a pedestal now felt like bleeding out on the inside. I faltered as
we encountered all the stop signs and potholes and old houses I'd seen
a million times. *This is it*, I said to myself. Twilight set in as we rode
past the old graveyard where Simon's engine had once idled and he
told me he didn't want any suitcases between us. Past the restaurant
with the chameleon names, past the barren lot where the Mercury
Diner once stood, past the bushes where Pete and I hid the first night
we played Spotlight. Traveling my hometown's geography at a crawling pace, I couldn't deny my own reflection. I *was* the graveyard, the
asphalt, the grass, the sky. We had done this together, the town and I.
More than Nora, who rode in a convertible ahead of me, more than
Pete or Simon, who had each performed their own homecoming rites,
Mercury itself had been my most loyal accomplice.

Even with all our failings, I belonged to this town and these people in a way I wasn't sure I could belong to anyone else. We shared the
same illusions, and we harbored the same secrets. As we crept through
town on the backs of American-made cars, the band playing, the kids
screaming, the fire trucks wailing, the mania swelled. It was real but it
was also a lie, and the whole town was besotted with it.

The only way a town of cinders could keep itself from dying out was to
set itself on fire again and again. After the parade wound down in the
high school parking lot, we gathered behind the school for the bonfire.
The group shrank as the sky darkened; only the most ardent Mustang
fans remained. By the woods, a heap of timber and cardboard had been
piled atop a patch of scorched earth, begging for a match. The football
coach held a megaphone to his mouth like a trumpet and yelled his
muffled pep talk to the team huddled around the blaze. The fans, the

court, and the town formed concentric circles around them. Somewhere, somebody beat a cowbell. One of the players struck the head of a match, and it burned as he tossed it onto the wood pile. In the deep heart of the fire, a flame glowed.

Out of the dark the cheerleaders emerged, sprinting toward it. Above their heads, they hoisted a life-sized cutout of a cartoon football player boasting our opponent's team colors. The football boys, charged now, yanked the cardboard cutout to have their way with it. They punched it, kicked it, and then pitched it in. I felt the heat on my face and opened my mouth to welcome the smoke. Fire, a savage assassin, reminded us all that we still had life left to lose.

The boys assembled into a hive, jumping in unison and chanting together. "MHS! MHS! MHS!" Flames danced on their faces as they screamed. In daylight they would have appeared excited, but in the dark smoke and flickering orange blaze, they just looked terrified instead.

The heat in Mercury continued to rise. A half hour before the Friday afternoon pep rally, those of us on the court were excused from class to make ourselves presentable to the gathering crowd. I changed my clothes in a stall of the junior high bathroom down the hall from the gymnasium. Hoping to approximate sophistication, I chose to wear all black.

Though classes were still in session, the whole school was too frothed to focus on academics. The other six debutantes from the homecoming court dressed themselves up as well, and a few escapees from class loitered along the perimeter. I stood in front of a tall, pocked mirror by the door and turned to the side.

"I look fat," I said to no one in particular.

"Oh, my God," one of the other girls on the court said. "Could you *be* any skinnier?"

I gave her a ready-to-wear smile before escaping to the other mirror above the bathroom sink. This one, also dented, showcased my face.

I leaned toward my reflection, which looked as it always did. Brown hair, green eyes, pale skin. I brought along a small arsenal of makeup that I didn't know how to use. Holding an eye pencil close to my tear duct, I paused, unsure what to draw first.

A fellow senior named Olivia—one who hadn't made it onto the court—stepped toward me.

"Here," she said. "Let me show you."

She used one index finger to pull taut the skin at the edge of her eye. Using her other hand, she penciled a fine line just above her lashes before releasing her finger.

"See?" Olivia said. "Easy. Pulling the skin makes it much easier. My mother taught me that."

Olivia had always been gorgeous. Dramatic eyes, a wide smile, and smooth, pale skin. When we were in junior high, Olivia had thick bangs and attended all the boys' basketball games with me as a fellow statistician. Since then, she'd become cheerleader with a part-time job on the side, leaving her without much time for schooling.

Five years ago on one of the many bus rides we took together to a junior high basketball game, she pulled a *Seventeen* magazine out of her bag and turned to a dog-eared page.

"NATION-WIDE MODELING CONTEST!" It screamed in bold letters. "THIS COULD CHANGE YOUR LIFE!"

"I'm going to enter," Olivia told me. "Want to see my photos?"

"Of course," I answered.

She unveiled her roll of film from its Rite Aid envelope. I looked through the photos. Olivia, lounging on a gray picnic table with one knee propped.

Olivia, in a tie-dyed mini-tee and cutoff jeans, lying on the pilling comforter of the bed in the room she shared with her sister.

Olivia up close, a beauty shot of her bright blue eyes and her bangs teased and sculpted to look like the leaves on a palm tree.

Olivia looked dwarfed among the emblems of her small house. Still, she was beautiful.

I looked back at the magazine to some of the faces that had already been chosen for the different categories. Somehow, all those girls had known to have their pictures taken against a blank backdrop.

I never heard how the contest turned out. Now, five years later, Olivia and I stood side by side again, back in the junior high wing.

"Thanks, Liv," I said, taking my eyeliner from her hand.

"Here, let me." Olivia leaned close to my face, her mouth barely open as she held her breath and outlined my eyes. When she finished, my eyes looked as dark as they had that Saturday afternoon at mime practice seven years ago, that moment I blended into the other girls with painted faces before I told the biggest lie of my life.

"There," Olivia said, pulling away. "Perfection."

At the pep rally, the gym beamed with electric orange. Cheese-colored floors, walls, and lights made an antsy crowd buzz in their seats. Seven chairs sat empty along the boundary line beneath the basketball hoop, waiting for seven girls to sit in them, one ankle delicately crossed over the other with her escort standing tall behind her. Each girl cradled a white carnation with a blue ribbon, and each couple stood for a moment beneath the glaring red EXIT sign, waiting to be called.

The voice booming from the PA system belonged to the speech coach, Mr. Hoskins. As we strolled in, Mr. Hoskins shared lists of our accolades and special interests. *Katie is a blue-ribbon winner at the 4-H and loves spending time with friends and family. Bob is a starting running back and likes to take his four-wheeler out on weekends.* The personal details had been published in a special issue of the school newspaper that had just been distributed so the audience could view the still pictures while catching the live show.

What's your favorite movie?
Your favorite saying?
Your favorite food?

When I filled out the interview sheet a few weeks before, Aaron had helped me with it. My favorite car? Aaron's car, a white 1989 Ford Tempo. My favorite game? Trivial Pursuit, Aaron's favorite game. As he looked at the sheet, Aaron let out his two-toned laugh. He thought homecoming was nothing more than a farce, and I desperately wanted to believe him.

"Tell me," he said. "What was your reaction to being named to the court?"

"Gee," I said, twirling a strand of my hair. "I hope the crown fits."

Aaron laughed. "Put it," he said.

"I can't. People will think I'm serious."

"Come on." His smile tempted me. "*Put it.*"

So I'd written it down, hoping everyone would be able to tell I'd meant it as a joke. But when Mr. Hoskins proclaimed it over the PA system, it sounded vain. *Too big for her britches,* I could almost hear the townsfolk whisper before Mr. Hoskins moved on to the next girl.

Before the pep rally concluded, the coach of the football team stepped up to the mike to give a final igniting hurrah to a team with many more losses than wins. He was impossible to understand.

Someone started the chant of M-H-S! M-H-S! The chanting trailed off as the hot, liquid crowd poured out of the gymnasium. Trying to sit demurely in my chair at the end of the basketball court, I did my best to fix a pasty smile where my mouth used to be.

On the evening of the homecoming game, the air was crisp as the sky turned golden mauve at dusk. I could see the setting sun beyond the football field, beyond the warehouses, beyond the distant trees that crowned the only home I'd ever known—a place that wanted to adore a young beauty as much as I wanted to be one. The marching band's snare drums snickered in the background. I waited with the other six girls near the chain-link fence for our escorts and convertibles to arrive.

One by one, we'd take our turns around the track that circled the football field; we'd present ourselves as evidence to the audience that our town, indeed, lived on:

Look, look at the girls Mercury has made. Seven girls in stockings and heels; seven girls with straight, white smiles; seven girls bracing in the wind.

Before I got into the car, I saw Aaron turn the corner by the fence and walk down the asphalt. In his arm, he carried a big bouquet of pink roses. He smiled when he handed them to me.

"Look at you," he said.

"I can't believe you came."

"Yeah, well." He shrugged.

Even more than the flowers, Aaron's presence was his true gift to me. I hadn't known it, but I needed him there. In a stadium packed with people who'd known me since birth, he was the only one who could part the sea of performance I swam in to find me—the real me—still breathing underwater.

The sunset melted into a steely lavender, the color of my convertible for the evening. The tires crunched over gravel before reaching the rubber track. I'd never been in a convertible before this week, and now I'd ridden in one twice. Sitting in it reminded me of Simon and how we flew down the hill in his jeep, my hair thrashing in the wind. But this car crawled around the field slower than a grandma, sluggish enough for everyone to get a good look. My name appeared in Magic-Marker bubble letters on a piece of poster board plastered to the side of the car, drawn by a girl who hadn't made it onto the court.

As we traveled to the far side of the field opposite the home stands, the noise dissipated and the night inked. It dressed my shoulders, my hair. I felt it in my lungs. The sky was cold and my ghostly breath revealed itself. These were the kinds of nights I'd fallen in love with a long time ago. They were why I never missed a football game, and they tempted to steal me away from my spiral staircase. Nights like this I couldn't imagine ever being anywhere else, in any other autumn, in any other town. Theirs was a beauty that stung.

The air was a concoction that could only exist here—the smell of rust and distant burning leaves. And it was beautiful. It was nothing but me and this sky, me and this chilling wind. I wanted to face it, bare myself to it. But in just a blink, there were all these people. All these eyes. All this watching. That night I wished for the impossible: to tell the truth and keep the lie, to stay and to leave, to take the town with me, the very thing I wanted to escape.

I knew there would never be another place as lovely as this one, as bleeding as this one, as fucking evanescent. The word "fuck" was created for a town like this—because it was beautiful and horrid and small and suffocating and contained everything precious to me. When Trent Reznor had written "Closer," I believed he could have been imagining a night just like this one when he had lived here. That's what it was to live in this town. It meant leaving this place because it was sick, and I didn't know how to save it.

The convertible dropped me off at the center of the home stands where a plywood platform had been built with seven chairs on top for the ladies to sit and watch the game. We posed for a few pictures, took our seats, and waited for halftime when the real show would begin.

My mind numbed and my eyes blurred as the game played out in front of me. Mr. Lotte's white house sat just a stone's throw away, on the other side of a stand of old trees, up the road from the only park in Mercury, and too far down the well of my memory for me to conjure it while the delirious crowd around me screamed for the young boys in blue to take what was rightfully theirs.

Just after Mr. Lotte's investigation ends and before his hearing begins, my father takes my brother Seth and me to Silver Pulley Park to fly a kite on a Saturday afternoon. After a long winter, the cold has finally broken and the trees shake their bare branches. There is an open, sloping field beside the public pool, just up the road from Mr. Lotte's white house, which sits at the end of a long, brown driveway that curls like the tail of a cat.

My father, brother, and I walk to the top of the hill where the ground levels out. We face northeast, toward the courthouse, Mr. Lotte's house at my back. I wear a pink jacket with a silver zipper, a pair of dark blue jeans. My father and brother stoop to untangle the long, white heap of string, and my father's fingers knead through it. His shoulders hunch as he kneels on the ground next to his son. A cold wind blows and I turn to look back down the hill toward the line of old maples growing fresh leaves that hide the house where I once waited in the balmy garage for Mr. Lotte to fetch me, sweat sliding down my back. The day it happened, I had come without my sister. She didn't need summer lessons every week to stay on track.

It was so hot that day. I wanted to be swimming. I saw particles of dust floating in the air from the light shaft coming in through the filmy window. The garage smelled like gasoline and leather. I stood next to his motorcycle, poised like a black puma on its kickstand. I held my piano books to my chest. The tinkling of muffled piano keys came through the basement door from the girl whose lesson was before mine. Outside the tiny garage window, the tops of the trees stood still. There was no wind like there is on the day my father hands me the blue-and-red kite, diamond shaped, made from vinyl and thin wooden rods. Even in my hands, the kite is so light that its back arches in the breeze, wanting to move with it. It pushes against my palm.

Seth clutches the end of the string and cracks it like a whip.

"Come on, Amy! Come on!" he squeals and jumps up and down.

There's a good wind, headed south. My father points to the far edge of the field and tells me to run toward it. I hear the soft pound of my sneakers as I run to the field's end while my brother yells, "Go, Amy! Go!" The ground gives way beneath my feet and I leave imprints in the wet, cool earth. When I reach the edge, I turn around and see my brother and father at the other end, the size of Nativity figurines. The rusty fence around the pool rattles.

My father instructs me to hold on to the kite as Seth runs in the other direction. I wait, just as I waited until the piano beyond the basement entrance stopped and the door opened. Mr. Lotte appeared, squinting at the light streaming through the glass. He held the door open for the girl, a few years older than me, who hobbled out on crutches. She had a thick white cast on her right leg, covered with graffiti signatures from her softball team, and her one flip-flop smacked against her left foot as she headed for the garage door. I held it open for her and waved to her mother, who got out of their minivan to take her daughter's book bag and help her inside the car.

I shut the door and turned around. It was just the two of us then, and I followed him inside. He slid the door shut behind me. How dark it was in the basement, how brown. Not black, not gray. Brown. Fake wood-paneling brown. Piano bench brown. His beard brown. Teabag brown. A single lamp glowed on the top of the piano, its light soft against the pale sheet music, as white as the pale spring sky thinly sheathed with clouds.

As my brother runs in the opposite direction, the string straightens and tightens. The kite flops from my hands and flutters against the ground. It hops jaggedly like a frog. Then the wind gets a good current beneath it and the kite puffs out its chest and begins its ascent. I clap. My brother squeals. My dad laughs. My father loves the wind, loves to drive with the windows down, to feel it pass through his fingers as he drives on Route 17 to and from town. Owning his own business leaves him with so few moments of release from the constant pressure, especially in a town where mills and jobs are vanishing. Work is scant for everyone. The kite keeps flying up and up and up, pirouetting through the sky. My father smiles and shields his eyes.

"Look at it," he yells so I can hear. "Look at that."

As I watch my father watching the kite, I know what love is. I do. I love the man who loves being my father. I never want to hurt him, never want him to hurt. I feel for the first time how sad and painful it can be to love someone so much.

I start walking back through the field toward my brother, toward the row of trees that keep me from seeing Mr. Lotte's house like no one could see me in his hot basement when I took a seat at the piano bench, the one with a flip-up top under which was a stock of old Christmas primers with staples eating away at the pages. Mr. Lotte made the same sound he always did when sitting beside me. Exhales and sniffs. The bench squawked in protest.

"Let's start with the warm-ups," he said.

I placed my fingers on the keys; he placed his hand on my back and turned on the black metronome with the flashing light. Tock tock tock tock. The red light blink blink blinked just as a plane does as it makes a diagonal through the blue sky. The blinking wings look like little red stars as our kite floats through the air.

Tock tock tock tock.

Don't I see it everywhere? Blinking wings of planes, radio towers, PRESS RESET buttons on the microwave, the alarm clock, the stove top when the power goes out?

(For so long I will tell myself, there's nothing there, there's nothing there, there's nothing there. But then, there is.)

The lazy Saturday afternoon passes and as I walk through the field, I stop at the fence and peer down into the empty pool bed. Inside three teen-aged boys are skateboarding down the slope into the deep end, and the rough sound of their wheels scraping against the floor catches in the wind. Black-hooded creatures floating through aquamarine. Wearing their dark colors, flowing so seamlessly, they look like dark birds in an inverted sky.

Far away, the taut string pulls against my brother's fingers and makes a sound so small he has to lean forward to hear it. There is an arch in the kite like the arch in my back as Mr. Lotte's hands wandered, scoured, discovered the landscape of my skin. His hand, sliding from the nape of my neck to the blade of my right shoulder to slip beneath my armpit, in search of some jewel in hopes of being the first to touch it. And he was.

It would only happen once, because the end was near. It would only happen in the smallest of movements, the lightest of sounds. How very, very slowly he approached forbidden territory, how very, very calculating, so that later I would ask myself, "Did he? No, it can't be. I must have imagined it."

A hand, innocent and wandering one moment, sinister and focused the next. How very, very quiet he was, the piano sounding its notes and I holding my breath like I held it on a safer summer afternoon when my sister had come along and I waited for her lesson to end. Mrs. Lotte and I leaned toward the television screen at the climax of the afternoon soap opera, squeezing the arms of our chairs, our lips barely parted like the sky parts from the sound of a skateboard skidding against sloping cement and the whoosh of a flying kite that Mr. Lotte can't see from the mouth of his curled driveway, from the corner of his lonely room, from the sill of his tiny basement window.

A few minutes before the second quarter ended, the girls on the court gathered at the fifty-yard line, each with her father in tow. That was part of the homecoming tradition. During halftime, the band created a tunnel, and each girl, like a young bride, was escorted down the fifty-yard line by her father while the PA system touted all of her favorite things. Last year's queen also got one final moment in the spotlight. She was the last to walk down the field before letting go of her crown once the new queen was named.

I'd been imagining this day since I was in junior high and witnessed my older girl-idols make this walk. Was there anything more regal than parading down a tunnel of gleaming brass trumpets and plumes lifted high? As my father and I promenaded arm in arm—he in a suit and turtleneck for the occasion—I couldn't bring myself to face the stares. The whole tunnel was constructed from unchosen seniors. As they played the notes to the homecoming ballad, I could feel their eyes travel with me when I passed. This is a sham, I should have told them, but my participation in it proved the opposite. I desperately wanted to be fooled, and not just about homecoming. I was sobering up to the fearful truth, even as I was intoxicated. My lie had protected me from outward harm, while inside I rotted. I had never felt young and beautiful. I had never felt young.

Every year, the announcer, Mr. Rhodes, got a thrill from holding the crowd hostage on homecoming night. This was his annual opportunity to receive undivided attention, and he knew how to milk it.

When the band resolved its final chord and the brass trumpets snapped down, the crowd quieted. It was an eerie feeling to watch a rowdy stadium fall silent, as if sound had thrown itself off a steep cliff. I knew people were staring at me, and I stared at the ground as we waited.

Mr. Rhodes began his yearly spiel.

And . . .

This year's . . .

New . . .

1998 . . .

Mercury High School . . .

Homecoming Queen is . . .

Senior . . .

Miss . . .

Andrea McCoy!

The crowd erupted. The rest of the court smiled and clapped as we swarmed around Andrea to congratulate her.

"It's all right," my dad whispered in my ear when I rejoined him. As my father smiled at me, I wanted to hold on to him and never let go. He squeezed my arm. "You don't want to have to repeat all this next year just to return the crown."

The rhinestones in Andrea's plastic tiara sparkled in the flash of a hundred cameras, and I realized my hands had lost all feeling a long time ago.

The Mustang fans only grew more frenetic after halftime. I thought the rest of the court would return to their plywood perches to watch the second half of the game, but the platform remained empty.

I hunted the stands for Aaron so he could remind me who I was apart from all this, but he'd gone. I figured he'd stayed as long as he could stand it, probably until after the announcement. I wished he'd waited for me. I wanted to go sit on the hood of his car in the dark, never mind my suit and heels. His 1989 Ford Tempo, buried somewhere in the mash of cars in the lot, with the two of us on top. That was how this night should have ended.

I just started to walk, acting like I was headed somewhere. Confetti filled the air and drifted like cinders. People still screamed as the game charged on. For the first time in months, I realized no one was watching me. It both relieved and unmoored me. In a sea of faces I recognized as well as my own, I felt like a stranger. I'd never felt so lost in my life.

The crowd turned tawdry, and the hoots and rollicks grew harsh as we all fell down the cold throat of another autumn in Mercury. For a moment I thought I could actually feel the world turning, even though I knew that was impossible because I was turning with it.

After homecoming, I knew what had to be done. No longer would I subject myself to faux desire or cloak myself in the imaginary because I feared what hid beneath it. During my final performance of *Bye Bye Birdie*, I slipped away during the last act. After sneaking into the public bathroom, I stepped into a stall and locked the door behind me. It was quiet, just like it was the year before when I'd drawn myself old in the same bathroom. I peeled off my leotard and tights, and they pooled at my ankles as I sat naked on the toilet.

I didn't have to go to the bathroom. Instead, I tilted my head to the right and rested it against the cool metal of the stall. The waistband of my tights had imprinted a thick red ring around my stomach. The sweat that dripped underneath the searing stage lights dried; a chill slid across my body and up the curve of my spine. Goose bumps. My skin coarsened and blotched.

I had repeated this ritual every year since I was a freshman member of the chorus, but this time was my last. And tonight was everything. Everything I'd been working for. It was an insular sensation—I didn't care about the audience or the actors or the pit band. I was the spotlight's object of affection, and it was mine. Now the time had come for me to release it, this shining light that had befriended me, guarded me, girded me, for as long as I'd needed it.

The door to the bathroom swung open and I heard the click-clack of high-heeled dancing shoes.

"Amy?" a voice called. "Amy Jo, are you in here?"

I said nothing. A silent moment passed before the door opened and shut. Alone again. In a few minutes I'd pull my leotard back on and head toward the stage for my final moment, but for now I waited on the toilet and inhaled. I loved that smell of dirt and sweat that clung to my leotard. It was the smell of work and passion and things that I loved. This was my postcoital high, and I smoked it like a cigarette.

*

Life after Mr. Lotte demands a certain kind of subliminal finesse, much like the manner in which a housewife plans a party. After a while, the formula melds to instinct: first you consider your guests, then your surroundings, and very last, yourself. It takes a great deal of effort to appear as if our actions require no effort at all, to clothe ourselves in the finest fabrics and swat away any attention we receive with, "Oh, this old thing?" Life is best when seen as a closet full of sparkling party gowns. It allows us to choose what to put on, what to cast off, and what to keep hidden away.

We start to orchestrate even the smallest part of our lives, from abandoning the snack line in the cafeteria to bringing our own lunches, packed in a crisply folded paper bag. We don't want to be seen waiting in line; we don't want anyone to know we have money in our pockets. We don't park in tight spaces. We don't loan out our books, and we never plan too far in advance.

We avoid situations where we'll be alone with older men. If a teacher wants to meet with us before or after class, we make sure we sit between him and the door. Every smart girl knows you first scan all the possible exits from a room before you sit down, cross your legs, and smile—even as your heart hammers away in your chest. Let your companion underestimate you, and then you'll gain the advantage. Interactions now have a currency to them, and if you aren't gaining shekels of prowess, you're paying them to someone else. It will take years to buy back all the ones Mr. Lotte took for himself.

And perhaps that's the biggest difference between B.L. and A.L. (Before Lotte and After Lotte). We've always been good girls, the best, forever eager to hide another's indiscretion and swallow it as our own. But Mr. Lotte has made us *smart* girls, too. Not that we'd thank him for it, if we could remember what he did to us. Instead, our actions take orders from a sheathed impulse to change the future because of the unknowable past. Never again will someone get the best of us. We believe in the Trinitarian gospel of good-girl survival:

1. The most cunning are disguised as the most naïve.
2. The sexiest word is no.
3. Speak well of everyone, and assume the worst.

The downside to our post-Lotte guide to survival is that we always feel as if we're in trouble. We suffer from guilty consciences, and we're counting down the hours until someone exposes us for our crimes. Every police car zooming past with glaring lights must be aiming to pull us over, even though we never speed. Every protracted stare from a man must mean he's deciphered our encrypted secrets. Every late night out is a regret waiting to happen; every letter carries bad news inside its envelope. Every first kiss is a prelude to loneliness.

This kind of life cannot continue forever. Perfection tamps the smolder of our hearts, and we're so very tired of the constant chill. One by one, our alarm clocks chime, and the awakening begins.

Origin Story

SOMETHING THAT WOULD ALWAYS be true: the young men in Mercury shone like constellations in a vast female sky. They were bright and piercing; we were endless and deep. Together, we drew a map that led toward the future and reminded us of the past. I needed those boys in Mercury not only to lay hold of my own hidden multitudes, but to see anew the place I would always be from. Pete and the myth of youth, Simon and the love of illusion, Aaron and the heart that still beat beneath the quiet wreckage.

Nine years before the night he brought me the homecoming roses, Aaron and I collided for the first time. On body-drawing day in third grade, our teacher Mrs. Steeple taught us the body was an agent of function, not feeling. The heart pumped the blood and the lungs pushed the air, each with its own circular rhythm. Now go and draw it, she said. Spread out in the barren auditorium, we turned our bodies into art.

With a crisp, clean sheet of drawing paper beneath me, I lay on my back with my hands splayed out, palms up. The outline of my body felt like a racetrack as my partner Melissa sped around it with a pencil. I liked the sensation of being traced. I felt at home in my body, a feeling I would chase for years to come.

I tilted my head to the right and saw a boy lying a few feet away from me, his hands outstretched like mine. He was just a regular boy, one who always bought a school lunch and got mud caked on his shoes at recess. Nothing to infatuate me. He closed his eyes as his partner sketched jagged lines around the perimeter of his body. His name was Aaron.

"Hold still," Melissa said. She dragged her pencil down the slope of my neck, off the cliff of my shoulder. "Finished," she said. "My turn."

I sat up while Melissa lay down. I traced her carefully, swirling a colored pencil around the corners of her elbows, the curve of her head. I dove into the valley between each of her fingers. Beside us, Aaron traced his partner and scooted around the edges of the paper as he drew. The dark rubber soles of his sneakers squeaked against the floor. His skin was almost as white as his socks. Like the synchronous, ticking minute hands of twin clocks, we revolved around our drawings.

Next we drew our organs into the white space of our bodies. I drew a duo of lungs that looked like butterfly wings. My heart looked like an apple. To add some flair, I drew glasses around my green eyes, a mole on my right cheek. A coil of thick bangs across my forehead and a waterfall of brown hair from the crown of my head to my shoulders.

I sat against the wall to examine the drawing of myself. I hadn't realized my head was so small. My butterfly wings leaned to the right. Aaron walked toward me, his dark blond hair extra fuzzy from lying on his back. He stood over me with his shoulders slightly hunched. His two front teeth had the tiniest sliver between them.

I looked up at him. "What?"

"I saw you picking your nose," he said.

"You did not," I said back.

"Did, too." His face remained calm, resolute. It made me mad.

"Did *not!*"

"Did. Too." The corners of his mouth crept into a smile. "You're lying."

"Go away, Aaron." I scowled. He laughed and ran away toward a group of boys bouncing a kickball. Their shoes screeched against the vinyl floor and the sound echoed across the auditorium.

Before the school day ended, we hung our drawings around our classroom, a clothesline of twenty-four white banners attached to the wall with Scotch tape. Each body, flat on its back, inside out. I spied Aaron's drawing. His irises were emerald green and his smile was a small, upturned parenthesis. His lungs looked like brown kidney beans, his heart a ball of bright red between them.

Since that day, I came to think of my friendship with Aaron as an item I possessed in a way I no longer possessed my own body, like a reel of film I could thread into an old-fashioned movie projector and watch it play. There was no sound, no need for words, only images in motion.

I saw him at Coyote's Pizza in his black half-apron, holding a tray with three plastic red glasses brimming with ice water. I saw him cower in a church pew, crimson-faced because his mother had rested her head on his father's shoulder during the sermon. I saw him hunch at a desk, penning his first editorial for the school newspaper: "Skipping School: What's the Big Deal?" I also saw him accept a perfect attendance award at the end of each school year. I saw him clench a guitar pick between his teeth as he pulled his guitar from its case. I saw his practiced thumb flip open the cap of a Zippo. I saw him smile and wave at me from behind the dashboard of his car.

If I stretched taut the film of us between my fingers and held it up to the light, I could see the two of us move in slow motion. It was 1999, the millennium was closing in, as was the diaspora of everyone I'd ever loved—people I knew so well that I could recite their mother's maiden names as well as their dead pets. I would never know anyone the way I knew these people, and I would never be known this way, either. In the final months of my youth, Aaron came to embody this paradox: it was possible to drown in both intimacy and anonymity. If I wanted to leave Mercury, I had to go alone. I couldn't take anyone with me.

For almost two months after mailing my application, I put all my escape plans on hold while I waited to hear back from Cornell University. I didn't let myself consider what would happen if I didn't get accepted. I knew I had two choices as I stared down the mountain of adulthood:

dig deeper into Mercury (and my lies and regrets hidden within) or escape, and I had chosen escape. Each day when I arrived at school, I opened my locker to find a picture I'd cut from a pamphlet of Cornell's clock tower, which stood right next to my hidden spiral staircase.

As the days passed, I grew worried. I should have heard by mid-December. "Relax," Aaron told me when he first saw me each morning. Then he repeated it in German class during the day's final period: "Give it a rest." I knew he was right. Still, I couldn't help but jet to the mail pile on the kitchen counter of my house each day after school to see if the letter had come.

On a dreary day in January, someone came to the door of my calculus class and handed a note to the teacher that summoned me to the main office.

I gathered my books and headed down the hall, wondering what they could want. Classes were still in session, and the corridor's silence hung over me. I hadn't gotten a note excusing me from class since Nora asked me to visit her in Yutes's office more than two years before. I'd never even gotten a detention. My father's face flashed in my mind. He spent most days climbing ladders and walking across rooftops. Had he fallen?

By the time I reached the office, I could barely breathe. When I went in, one of the school secretaries—Mrs. Bonner, a good friend of my mother's—shut the door behind me.

"Your father called," she said.

"Is it my grandparents?" I asked. "Are they all right?"

"Everyone's fine," she said.

I exhaled.

"I have good news," she said. "Your dad said he just couldn't wait for you to get home from school, so he opened a letter that came for you from Cornell."

My heart stopped. "And?"

Mrs. Bonner stood up. "You got yourself into an Ivy League school, young lady."

Never had the building around me felt so hopeful. "I *did?*"

"You did."

"I *did?*"

"You did!"

I'd done it, and the thrill I felt was greater than I'd imagined. Joy zipped through my entire body. That inner heat that had lain dormant too long inside me started to blaze. I'd done it. After years of hiding in the spotlight, I had finally found a path that promised to lead me back to myself.

By March, most of my friends had found their escape routes as well. Many had been accepted at local colleges, some enlisted, and one even gotten into West Point. Though not all would follow through, everyone at least planned to get out of town. Everyone except for Aaron, who didn't have any plans at all.

"You're smart, Aaron," I told him one morning in journalism class. "You should apply to Slippery Rock. It's cheap and you could still work at Coyote's if you want to."

The two of us stood side by side in front of a small desk as we arranged the layout for the next issue.

"Besides," I continued as I paginated the sheets. "It might be too late already."

Aaron's face was blank. "I can't pay for it."

"My dad said he'd help you apply for financial aid."

He frowned. "You talked to your dad about it?"

I looked up at him. "I thought you could use the help."

He didn't respond, so I kept pushing. A wedge was growing between me and my friend: this place wasn't enough for me, and he knew it. I was leaving, and I wanted him to leave, too. Then I'd be leaving less of what I loved behind.

"Come on, Aaron," I said. "You don't want to work at Coyote's for the rest of your life, do you? Don't you want to get out of here?"

He pressed his palms into the table and turned his head toward me. "Honestly, I don't think it matters much where I end up."

I hated when he talked about himself that way, as if the end had already been written. But I didn't want to argue with him anymore. We finished our work in silence as the spring wind shook the trees in Mercury. Paralyzed by the coming ritual of departure, both our hearts were prone to linger where they shouldn't.

In April, things in Mercury headed toward a fever pitch, and we awaited the moment after which nothing would ever be the same. There were so few of them, after all. Birth. Death. First love. Leaving home. We'd seen so many before us not disappear, but turn invisible. Every last rite felt too much like death, like whispering final prayers while looking down the barrel of a gun.

The spring delirium that struck our town came from a different stock than our beloved Friday night football. It didn't stem from idolatry, but manic boredom, the need for something—anything—to *happen*, an event we couldn't predict. Kids so close to graduation were dropping out like flies. *Gonna go drive a truck*, some of them said. *I got my CDL and they're gonna pay me six hundred bucks a week.* Who could pass up an opportunity to drive into the night, to leave Mercury behind again and again, always to return?

As spring passed, prank bomb threats bloomed along with the daffodils. The joker took care to cloak his identity; he dialed the main office from pay phones (using, perhaps, the very one in the main hall of the school) and made his conversations quick. All it took was one word—BOMB—and the faculty evacuated the entire school. A paradox: the threat of demolition on the sunniest of days. Something about this tension made me feel green inside, confessional, as if I might be made new within the old skin of this small town.

These bomb-threat afternoons waned in a divine concoction of lazy idleness and provocative fear. The thought of witnessing the school before us explode into fire and rubble was seductive. It would be majestic and horrible, just right for the class of 1999 to make its exit. The prank caller never had any intention of setting off a bomb, but it didn't matter. He understood that in Mercury, appearance was paramount. The possibility of a threat was all we needed to get a little buzz.

On one of these wasted afternoons, Aaron and I sat on the hood of his car, just as we always did, a river of inane conversation flowing between us. Why his hands always smelled like onions, how long it would take to get across town if you scored all green lights, and if it really was possible to reach the center of a Tootsie Pop only by licking it.

Our conversation flitted among topics, landing on what Ithaca might be like in the fall. Aaron was the only person who knew that I was as scared to leave as much as I wanted to go.

"There will be so many people," I said. "I've never really had to meet new people before."

"You'll be fine," Aaron said. "There will be a ton of guys waiting to ask you out."

I laughed. "I doubt it."

"I'm serious," he said.

"I want them to." I had stopped thinking—why think when the air smelled so clean and this building might blow into so many pieces it could never be put together again? I let the words spill out of me. "So I can reject them."

Aaron's laugh sounded its high-low notes, but I could tell he didn't think it was funny. I never quite knew how Aaron felt about me, and I liked it that way. He was careful about laying his feelings bare, and I liked leaving things unsaid. Lately, I'd felt our relationship bucking, trying to free itself from my grip.

Those words belonged to a colder version of myself, the one I used to get what I wanted, the one I needed to hide my worst secrets. I didn't know where the thought had come from, but I knew an uncomfortable, unsolicited truth had just slipped out. Honesty, I was learning, bowed to no one. Aaron examined me with a troubled expression, and I couldn't tell if I'd just confirmed what he already knew to be true, or if he'd just realized that he didn't know me at all.

On the night of the prom, 1999 had never felt so neon-bright. Aaron was my date, and I let him drive my car for the first time. The night became a supernova, and the golden lights against a navy sky made romance appear where it hadn't been before. Throughout the evening, my body orbited Aaron's. As we traveled side by side with windows down and the wind pushing in, we laughed. At a stoplight, I took a picture of Becca and her date, who were driving in the lane alongside ours. Aaron's hazy profile appeared along the outermost edge of the shot. He looked relaxed as we remained concentric, a safe distance apart as we circled Mercury's outer limits.

But the optimism of the evening quickly dissipated. This life we led was all imaginary, and it was about to expire. At the dance, Aaron seemed to close in on himself. I maintained my orbit, all the while keeping him as my beacon. He danced, he talked, he sat, he ate. Regarding him from varied distances, he seemed to be working hard at feigning happiness. I'd never seen him fake anything in his life. Why now? When I came near, Aaron retreated. He looked away, stepped toward the door, and pulled his hands behind his back.

During the evening's final dance, his body felt rigid next to mine. He looked past me, keeping his eyes on the parquet dance floor. It felt like dancing with a scarecrow.

"Are you all right?" I asked. Finally, he looked at me. I wasn't used to seeing his face so close to mine. His eyes had bags under them.

He gave me a half smile. "I'm fine," he said.

"Have you been sleeping?" I asked.

"I've just had a few late nights, that's all."

We continued to dance, our bodies unyielding. He maintained a set distance between us, which he'd never done before. Out of curiosity, I leaned my chin into his shoulder. He pulled away.

After the dance, a few friends of ours rented a hotel room at the Super 8 Motel by the outlet mall. Aaron had said he wanted to go, and I agreed even though I wasn't much for crowds or parties. We rode quietly in the dark, listening to the radio. When we pulled into the motel's vacant lot, Aaron shut off the engine but neither one of us got out of the car.

I waited for his hand to leave the wheel. Around us, the gleam of the lampposts shone like the beam of a flashlight on the grid of the empty parking lot. The face of the hotel had a hundred lit eyes that poured glazed light into the dark. With the windows up, the air inside the car was thick.

"You don't want to go in, do you?" I asked.

He shrugged. "Do you?"

I shrugged back.

"I think we should call it a night," he said. "It's late."

I frowned. Eleven-thirty might have been late for me, but it was early for Aaron. I turned toward him.

"What's wrong?" I asked. "Didn't you have a good time?"

"I'm fine. I had a great time."

Aaron hardly ever used the word "great." For the first time, he had lied to me and I couldn't understand why. I thought about my ugly confession on the hood of his car not so long ago. Maybe Aaron had seen the real me, and he didn't like it.

"Nothing's wrong?" I asked.

"Nothing."

The engine turned, and the impulse to grab him around the neck almost overtook me. Not to choke him or kiss him, but to keep him. I stayed my hands at my sides as he merged onto the main road. I realized then the hard truth I'd been avoiding. When I left Mercury, it would be a clean break. If I kept looking back to this place I loved, regret would devour me. Standing on my empty driveway, watching Aaron's car disappear, I feared that I was about to lose everything precious to me.

———

The last time we sat on the hood of Aaron's car, he was jonesing for a cigarette. It was humid and the air smelled like hot tar and automobile exhaust. From the asphalt parking lot, we watched the track team run drills around the football stadium. School had just let out, and horns beeped. Whistles blew. The rusty fence in front of us jangled in the wind.

I knew he wanted to smoke because he flipped his Zippo open and shut. Like the valves of a heart, it opened and shut. The top of it snapped back with the flick of his thumb. I knew he wouldn't smoke in front of me because he never did. I knew Aaron. He was always honest. He loved this place. He thought that I didn't. He'd never speak of this conversation again after it was over. It wasn't his style.

Graduation was close, and talk of leaving town was closer. We all dreamed of getting out and eluding the betrothed epitaph: "Born here. Lived here. Died here." Some of us would escape it, and some of us wouldn't. I had my ticket out, and Aaron wasn't interested in buying one.

I heard the friction of a metal wheel scraping against flint. We watched the blue inner flame consume the air that would have held the ash of the cigarette he wasn't smoking, the breath of the words we weren't speaking. This was it: the moment after which nothing would be the same. If I was nothing more than a wick, I'd turn to smoke at the strike of Aaron's match. But first, I'd burn.

"I've been seeing someone," he said. Open and shut. "I thought you should know."

The earth stopped on its axis, but not because I didn't want Aaron to find a cure for his chronic loneliness. It was because I knew that cure would replace his need for me.

"How long?" I asked.

"About a month." Open and shut.

"Who is she?"

He paused and winced, though I knew the wince was meant for me. "She's older," he said.

A sharp whistle trilled from the football field. My mouth had gone dry. All this time, he'd kept it a secret. I opened my mouth to speak, but he interrupted me.

"I know you don't approve. Just promise me you'll keep it a secret until we graduate. She could get in real trouble. Just do it," he said. "For me."

Aaron stared at me with tight lips, a tense brow. I realized he was holding his breath. I felt sick. He had found his own way of moving on before it was time, and the reality rocked me. Leaving Mercury had become my lover, and I was consumed by it. My life depended on my exodus. I needed to get out of this town, and Aaron needed to stay. The origin of me meant the end of us.

"Promise me," he said.

"I promise."

He exhaled. "Thank you."

A soft wind passed and rattled through the fence gate. I leaned back. Aaron leaned back. A plane passed overhead on its way to Pittsburgh. If anyone from above looked down on us, the soft eggshell of his car, bright as a clean piece of drawing paper, would stand out against the dark asphalt like a black-and-white frame from a movie reel. From above, they'd see us, leaning back on the hood of his car. Our outlines, side by side, would burn into the backs of their eyelids. After they passed and for the moments before the plane began its descent into the Steel City, they'd close their eyes and see an imprint of Aaron and me and our empty-beer-bottle hearts, palms up, looking into the sky.

If I wanted to live my life, I had to let Aaron live his. For the period of time I'd needed him most, Aaron had been the one to truly *see* me when I couldn't even see myself. In spring, before the bomb threats, before the prom, and before I left for good, I gave Aaron my yearbook and asked him to write something for me.

"Write something funny in it," I said.

He took it and kept it for over a week.

"What's taking so long?" I asked him after he'd had it for three days.

"I'm working on it, okay?"

"Fine, fine," I said, and I waited.

Yes, Aaron had been the one to see me, but he'd also allowed himself to be seen. He taught me that a quiet baring of oneself didn't have to invite harm. It could be beautiful instead. On one of the summer afternoons Aaron and I spent together in West Virginia, the group of us from Pure Heart Presbyterian went for a long, steep hike to the top of Seneca Rocks. When we reached the top, the view gave us endless, rolling slopes of evergreen. They were soft and elegant like the curves of a nude woman's back. We all stood in a row, catching our breath and inhaling the view. We sweltered in the heat. Aaron took off his shirt, wiped the sweat from his forehead, and bent over with his hands on his knees. His pale back had even strokes of purplish-blue on it, almost like a ribcage. The sides of his chest expanded and contracted as he breathed, and the strokes grew and shrank.

"Aaron, what happened to your back?" I asked.

He stood tall and faced the valley. "They're stretch marks," he said, pulling his damp shirt over his head. From then on, he swam with a shirt on. That kind of nakedness, however momentary, inspired reciprocity. I'd remember it years later as I gathered the strength to tell the truth about my own life.

When Aaron finally returned my yearbook, his message filled an entire page. At the end, he wrote:

I hope I have done half as much for you as you have done for me. You have really been something special to me and I will miss you when you become rich and famous and move to China or Japan or wherever else you want to go, and when I become a famous rock star. If you want I'll get you backstage passes and you can come to all of my shows.

I'm sorry I burned you at camp when we were CITs. I don't know what I was thinking. Anyone else would still hate me, but you forgave me in a limited amount of time. Save that song I gave you and when I do become a rock star you can sell it, but you will already be rich and famous so you might want to hold onto it.

Love,

Aaron

The song he mentioned was one he'd composed himself. *For you*, the paper had read when he handed it to me. The song was about the lengths we go to for those we love. Maybe one of the reasons Aaron and I understood each other so well was because we each had our secrets, and we were learning the art of coming clean.

♪

We kept your secret, Mr. Lotte. We kept it. You were forty-eight and had tea breath. We had perms and sunburns. You took more than your fair share of the piano bench, and we wore sleeveless shirts. You had an affinity for dull pencils, and we couldn't read your handwriting. Your house smelled like green beans. You told us to close our eyes and gave us Hershey's kisses. We kept our shoes on so our feet could reach the pedals. You never said our names. We knew there were prettier girls.

Each spring, we practiced our pieces for the recital. Some of us performed well, others of us kept striking the same sour chords. You turned our pages. You clapped. You told us we had no reason to be nervous.

In summer, we took lessons to improve. Some of us did, and some of us never practiced. We swam every day, and we came with wet hair. We handed you five-dollar bills out of our parents' wallets. We watched soap operas with your wife. We knew it was impolite to make fun of your fat fingers.

Often, your hand drowsed on our thighs while the beat hypnotized you. Slow down, your hand said. Speed up. You patted the smalls of our backs. Then our spines. Then our shoulder blades. Then our chests. You followed your own sheet music. We kept playing, because you had created a league of girls who were consummate performers.

Later, you got sick. It would be kind to say you were portly. It would be honest to say you were fat. You needed to drop some weight, Mr. Lotte. You dropped some students instead. When some of us heard, we dropped our ice cream sandwiches. You chose Leah. You chose Monica. You chose Annie. You didn't choose us, and you never told us why. We passed you in the school hallway, and you said nothing.

In fall, we heard the rumors about you. The police came to our houses. They asked questions. We lied. You weren't guilty. Then you were. We won spelling bees and the hearts of young men. You got one year. We didn't feel sad or feel regret. We didn't feel. We didn't want this to be about you.

You disappeared. You returned. You shopped at the grocery store. You went to the bank. You ate out. You kept your beard. You kept your wife. You found a different job. You took up space. You let the metronome battery die. You played your piano alone.

We forgot you. We got our braces removed. We got phone calls and did a thousand pirouettes. We drew hearts over our *i*'s. We learned about photosynthesis. We learned how to win at euchre. We stopped swimming so much. Some of us rode in convertibles for the homecoming parade. Others of us cried in bathroom stalls. We moved away. We came back. We didn't want this to be about you. We, the ones who lied, never spoke to one another. We are still in disguise, and we wonder why the past bothers us still.

When the time for telling the truth had long since passed, we remembered the wiry red flecks in your beard. The squared bottoms of your teeth. We remembered the weight of your palm and the squeak of the basement door. We remembered squeezing the handle of your motorcycle in the garage. We remembered saying no, officer, no. No he didn't. And we remembered that yes, Howard, yes. You did.

We felt the need to tell someone. But it was so long ago. We called hotlines, we shut off our cable. We took up running. We grew out our nails. We cut our hair and found therapists. Some of us confessed that we couldn't stop eating Cheetos for breakfast. Others of us confessed our sins to one or two of the seven girls and asked for forgiveness. Somehow, they understood.

Now we sleep with the fan on. We cry when we listen to country music. We use well-sharpened pencils. We worry about buildings tipping over. We put too much salt on our popcorn. We miss home most in autumn. We keep our eyes closed underwater. This is about you, isn't it?

We hold our breath when we drive past your house. Some of us don't play piano anymore. Others of us play the opening riff of *Fame* at parties. It depends. Some of us are no longer here to see you walk through town. Others are around to see people wave. Some people now claim they always knew there was something off about you. Others still think you were set up by a group of ten-year-old girls. Most don't remember what happened anymore. It was so long ago.

We did it. You never asked, but we kept your secret, Mr. Lotte. We kept it.

Cinderland

ON MY LAST NIGHT AT SUMMER CAMP, we set our sin on fire. As the sun sank over Lake Erie, the sky turned marigold and violet against the water's silvery expanse. The campground fell quiet as the other counselors, campers, and I took our flashlights and made the slow hike up to the far hill's highest point. The outdoor chapel overlooked the shallow valley, and as we filed into the ten rows of stone pews chiseled into the hillside, the trees cast their charcoal outlines onto the grass below.

The air held a silken chill, much like the feeling I used to get when emerging from the Silver Pulley pool on an overcast day. A chill that wouldn't hang around long enough to grow cold. The soft twang of Aaron's guitar floated through the air as he tuned the strings. I sat in the middle of the crowd, watching his fingers move, his body a shadow against the backdrop of the summers we'd spent together. I wondered if I'd ever be as close with anyone else as I was with him. His expression, still and reserved, could have been dismissed as blank by someone who didn't know him as well as I did. He was pensive, careful. Removing a pick from his pocket, he strummed through the opening chords of "Sanctuary," a song we'd sung almost every summer camp night for the past four years. G chord–A chord–D chord.

Our voices came together, timorous and somber. When we'd first sung this song together, we were young. We felt young, running through the woods with our flashlights. The first night I'd slept beneath the stars had been at camp seven years ago with the friends who surrounded me now. At the end of that summer, Mr. Lotte started his prison sentence.

But I didn't think of him as I lay beneath the stars, my sleeping bag getting damp from the grass beneath it. Instead I looked upward, feeling safe as the church boys chased each other in circles around me.

Now, though I wasn't yet eighteen, I knew I'd grown too old for this town. It had happened during my final performance on the MHS auditorium stage, seated among my classmates dressed in slippery blue commencement gowns, as we took our hats and tossed them in the air. A hundred caps rising, peaking, and falling to the floor. If I returned to this campground next year, I'd be an anachronism. I would no longer belong in a place I once called home. In Mercury, you were either young or you'd aged too fast. On to another life, I'd never find this kind of quiet intimacy again.

After a few choruses, Aaron resolved the melody and the chaplain came to the front. He opened his Bible to the gospel of John and started to preach from it. The Gospel, he said, meant "the good news." And "sin," he said, came from the verb "to miss." We had all missed the mark.

Even as a camper, I'd always loved this final night of camp. This land, these stars, even the gray, frigid water always seemed to wash me clean. All the other nights of the year, I fell asleep with my guilt lying next to me. After burying Mr. Lotte's transgressions, I couldn't find the guilt's origin any more than I could deny its presence. Years later, I'd trace the shame back to a trinity of antecedents: I'd lied about Mr. Lotte, I'd abandoned the other girls who told the truth, and though I confessed the sins I committed, I wasn't sure if I fully regretted them. I knew I'd make the same choices if given the chance, and it was a fault I couldn't reconcile. What I would learn to do, in time, was to own the pain that Mr. Lotte had caused. Not just to my body, but a pain that cut deeper when he'd allowed me to betray myself. For so long, I denied myself the right—the need—to grieve it. When I finally did, I welcomed the hurt. After years of silence, it was finally mine.

Before the evening's vespers service began, each of us had taken a small white candle from a beat-up cardboard box. At the sermon's close, the chaplain lit his candle with a match, then offered his flame to the person sitting at the end of the first row. That candle lit another, then another, than another, just like those boys who lit their hands on fire just down the hill from the chapel three years ago.

Those boys I'd grown up with, those church boys, all sat around me now. Teddy, who kept swatting mosquitoes. Hoyce, whose cherubic face turned impish when he smiled. Mikey, who never lost his baby fat. We had a habit of sticking together, but we were about to break it. Tonight was the last time we'd sit together like this. Most of the boys were staying local, going to school somewhere close by. Aaron was still undecided.

Hoyce leaned toward Mikey, tipping his candle so the hot wax dripped on his arm. Mikey elbowed him in the gut. Their stifled snickers were barely audible over the slow plucking of an old guitar.

The service ended with a hundred candles hoisted in the air and a tepid a cappella rendition of "Pass It On," a song we all hated but sang anyway because undoubtedly, one of the older church lady counselors would be overcome with emotion and couldn't help but belt out the first verse. We weren't the kind to leave her hanging.

After the final vespers service, some of the other counselors and I decided to introduce a new ritual to our campers. We took them to the blazing campfire at the edge of the property by the cliff that led to the shore of Lake Erie, the same spot where Aaron had once spied Simon and me in the dark. The kids crowded around the fire, a few lucky ones snagging the four or five tree stumps as seats. Each camper wore the same beaded bracelet he or she had made in craft time earlier in the week. Every leather cord held five colored beads, each color a symbol of salvation.

Yellow	Black	Red	White	Green
God	Sin	Jesus	Forgiveness	Life

That afternoon, Becca and I had torn about thirty thin strips of paper, and we handed them out around the fire. I held my own tiny strip of paper in my palm. It felt light enough to float away. Someone passed around a box of mismatched pencils, and I stepped toward the flames.

With his guitar slung around his shoulder, Aaron stood nearby. Aaron had always stood nearby. He'd only known me as Amy Jo, just a girl, not the performer's persona I constantly tried to inhabit. The current strain on our relationship lessened the blow of the distance about to span between us, almost as if we'd done it on purpose. Holding resentment had become our means of separation. He'd found the girl he was going to marry. I was sure of it. I knew she wouldn't let him go. I had no place in their future together, and Aaron didn't need me anymore. Around the fire, he started to run his pick against the strings of his guitar.

"We all have sins we hold onto," I said to the campers. I felt the flames' quick heat on my cheeks. "Let's write those sins on a piece of paper, toss them into the fire, and watch them burn."

My words were met with silence and bowed heads. I caught flickers of faces aglow from firelight. Hoyce, who had dribbled candle wax on Mikey just a half hour ago, was the first to drop his paper into the flames. One by one, the campers did the same.

Though I was leading this ceremonial expulsion of sin, I couldn't bring myself to release my strip of paper. I felt shame for a myriad of things. I feared the icy heart I thought was to blame for my wanting to leave the only place I'd ever called home, a place I loved like my own family. I didn't know what to write. Carly. Nora. Aaron. Pete. We'd all lost each other on our quests to get out of town, in our choices to remain. That was how the game was played, right? In our prisoner's dilemma, even the winners lost.

I thought my cold heart was beyond saving, but in time I would come to see what a lie that was. My heart was only restless, searching for a place to lay itself down for a while. Yes, I had missed the mark. I had remained silent when I should have spoken. I failed my town, my friend, and myself. And yet somehow, all this had been the very making of me, the friction I needed to push beyond the borders that penned all of us in. Out of the lie, a truer version of myself came to life.

That night in Erie, I was years away from being able to capture something so monumental on a scrap of paper. Instead, I wrote down some innocuous misdemeanor—a tiny indiscretion I'd no longer remember the next day. Even though I know I must have written something down, in my memory that small strip of paper remains blank. It seems right to remember it that way, the clean white paper not just a symbol for the silence that enveloped me, but a promise for the coming day when I would no longer be haunted by my past regrets.

For a long time, I'd done my best to keep myself in line. I hated the feeling of shame and regret, of missing the mark. I'd felt that way ever since I was five years old, when I attended kindergarten at a private Christian school three days a week. My teacher, Mrs. MacMillan, used to give us blue pens to use in our coloring books instead of crayons. It made me dislike her. After getting into a car accident, for weeks she perched stiffly in her teacher's chair, her chin resting on a big piece of foam. Her rigid neck seemed to make all of her other joints rigid, too. She moved around like she was made of Popsicle sticks.

I liked to use my pen to draw stars and hearts on my printing paper next to the questions I answered correctly. Mrs. MacMillan liked to grab my hand. "Now is not the time for drawing stars and hearts," she would say.

One night I woke up in a panic because I did not have my Bible verse memorized for that week. We were working our way through the alphabet, learning a verse that began with each letter. That week we'd come upon the letter *V.* The verse, written on an orange card, hung on the chalkboard in class. All week I'd been trying to memorize it.

"Verily, verily, I say unto you, he that believes in me has everlasting life." John 6:47

I closed my eyes. *Verily verily I say*—. I opened my eyes. *Verily verily, I say unto you*—.

Verily. What is a verily? Someone's name. That must be it. A Bible verse for someone named Verily.

I couldn't take the worry, so I climbed out from under my covers and ran down the hall to the living room where my parents were reading on the couch.

"I just can't remember it," I cried. "I just can't." I kept trying to put one word next to another, like train cars. But I didn't know what they meant. Verily. Everlasting. What were these words?

My father peeled an orange and gave me some of its wedges. My mother rubbed my back and repeated the verse with me until I finally memorized it.

I inhaled.

VerilyverilyIsayuntoyouhethatbelievesinmehaseverlastinglife. John6:47.

I exhaled.

"See? There's nothing to worry about. You knew it all along," my parents said and smiled, though they both looked concerned. They put me at ease, they put me to bed. The next year, they put me in public school. Even before Mr. Lotte, I had chased my own perfection. That memory of the Bible verse always made me picture the letter *V*, the shape flocks of birds adopt when making their escape.

After scribbling something on my strip of paper, I stepped toward the fire and squinted as I peered into it. The crowd behind me had grown bored with the ceremony; they were ready for the solemn portion of the evening to conclude. Still, the fire drew me toward it, the perfect blend of yellow and red, the beaded color of God and Jesus mixed together.

F. The letter F. For all have sinned and fall short of the glory of God. Romans 3:23

I. The letter I. In all thy ways acknowledge the Lord and the Lord will direct thy path. Proverbs 3:6

R. The letter R. Renew a right spirit within me. Psalm 51:10

E. The letter E. Except the Lord build the house, they labor in vain who build it. Psalm 127:1

I let the piece of paper slip from my fingers and watched it shrivel and blacken as it turned from what *is* to what *was*. I could think of no better rite of passage. The dark ash of everyone's iniquities filled the air. The smoke stung my eyes. The soot of our sins dispersed, just as we were about to.

Below us at the bottom of the cliff, gray water lapped against pale sand, a soft liquid voice that sang us to sleep each night. I felt it, what my mother must have felt when she was young and decided to leave home. I made a decision to follow with blind faith the one steady command inside me: *leave, leave, leave.* But no matter where I went, I'd never be able to separate myself from the hometown, both infinite and mortal, both angel and demon, that formed me.

That evening, our last evening together, we sat around a flaming pile of wood set beneath a wash of meager stars, an open sanctuary of sin. Here, we were ephemeral kings and queens by our own estimation, broken boughs our scepters and red plastic cups our chalices. Soon the fire died, the little bits of paper too quickly consumed to sustain it.

Fire had fascinated me ever since the moment I first witnessed some-one tame it. Picture this: a row of burning candles lined the middle of the buffet at a church Christmas banquet. In the dark, they resembled a string of shiny buttons sewn into the back of a woman's black dress. The lip of the buffet table reached just above my five-year-old chest. On my tiptoes, I slipped my left hand into a pair of tongs and began to chase after a tomato that kept slipping through the metal.

My father stood across from me on the other side of the table. His right hand, strong from the hours he spent installing roofs, nimble from pressing the strings of his guitar, reached across the buffet table and dug the tongs into the lettuce, heaping some of it on my plate. I felt embarrassed that I needed help. Being left-handed, I had difficulty imitating the ways other people maneuvered things like pencils, scissors, and shoelaces. I often led with my left foot instead of my right in ballet class and tended to pirouette in the wrong direction.

My father's arm stretched across the table for a moment as he let go of the tongs. The metal clanged against the side of the salad bowl. I remember the cuff of his dark wool sweater and the brightness of the candelabra's flame in the dark. The flame latched onto his sleeve and snaked up his arm, around his neck, and down the other arm.

The woman beside my father in line yelled, "That man's on fire! That man's on fire!"

There wasn't time to panic. Thin like a blade, the seam of fire surrounded him, setting my father's top half ablaze.

He dropped his plate, and it stuttered against the table. He grabbed the bottom edge of his sweater and whipped it off, smacked it against the ground and the flame went out in an instant. The sweater sat in a heap on the floor. He grunted slightly. The room was quiet. Then he picked it up and inspected it. The wool was dark and the room was dim. The sweater looked just as it had before it caught fire, like nothing had happened. My father put the sweater back on, returned to the line and finished filling his plate.

I'd seen and heard of this sort of magic before. The prophet Isaiah had once said, "When you walk through fire, you will not be burned." I'd also seen female baton twirlers in parades, of which Carly was one, how they threaded their fire batons through their fingers and in between their legs as if made from wax. Carly, I thought, was indestructible. How wrong I had been, I who had witnessed her destruction.

I remember how still I stood in the church sanctuary. I watched the offending cranberry-colored candle drip wax onto the white table cloth. My father, a roofer, musician, potter. A fire tamer.

My father spent much of his life walking atop Pittsburgh's industrial skyline. He was on a roof in the early morning before the summer sun rose and the temperature peaked. He was there at night in pitch black conducting infrared tests. He dropped his cellphone from a roof into a river below. From this view, he witnessed his city expand, thrive, struggle, and shrink. He watched it grow old and give way to what was sleeker, faster, richer. Still, he loved it just as much as his father and his father's father had. And that was why he chose to stay. He remained faithful to the city in times of feast and famine.

I did not want to tell this story. I can picture the broad-shouldered men who used to work in town: spreading asphalt in the summer, hunting buck in the winter. I can hear them say, *Shut your goddamn trap, will you?* Not because they feel the need to keep secrets, but because they still believe in the innocence of a man I once protected.

Who do you think you are, anyway? they'd say. *You hightailed it outta here the first chance you got. Some hotshot you are.*

And they'd be right. My memories of this place are cinders floating in the air. Levis. Cheerleader skirts. Bonfires. Gravel. Four-wheeler accidents. A ticking piano metronome that mimics the constant ticking of a clock. The road that leads home is flanked with clusters of white-washed, wooden crosses: memorials for the dead that have been erected by those who are still asleep.

This was my life on the outskirts of the Steel City. At times, people's minds were like abandoned steel mills, filled with nothing but ghosts. We were kids growing up in the Rust Belt in a city past its prime. We knew what it meant to be born into the white of the dandelion, how to live life in a dying place.

Yinz keep telling us that the Steel City ain't what it once was, but just you wait. Nothing ain't worth nothing unless it gets broke down and forged in fire.

I still tend to put words together like train cars—words like obey and rebel, exodus and return. City limits, country roads. I try to sound them out, make them new. Make them mine.

This is a rusty city past its peak, some may say. But set us on fire and see that we will not burn. Look inside us and see that we are made of steel and water and other immortal things.

Acknowledgments

First, to my agent, Meredith Kaffel, who is as wise, insightful, and compassionate as anyone I've ever met, thank you for being the perfect advocate and a dear friend. You saw something in my work that had yet to be born, and you found a way to pull it out of me. Amy Caldwell, thank you for loving this book and giving it a wonderful home. The amazing Beacon team—Helene Atwan, Pam MacColl, Tom Hallock, Will Myers, Melissa Nasson, Susan Lumenello, Marcy Barnes, Jane Gebhart, and Bob Kosturko—thank you for getting behind this book with such heart and enthusiasm. Kate Garrick and Morris Shamah at DeFiore & Co., many thanks for your hard work and expertise.

To all of my Hunter classmates, thank you for sharing your lives and your work with me. Each of you gave me such courage. Lia Ottaviano and Samantha Smith, who read this book from its first words to its final draft, thank you for pushing me, challenging me, and loving me. Much love also to Krystal Sital for always calling at the right time. To my readers Janna Leyde and Jeannie Vanasco, thank you for examining my work with a keen memoirist's eye. I'm indebted also to Rosy Kandathil and Amber Kelly-Anderson for their important last-minute assistance. Scott Cheshire, thank you for your advice on all things writing and life. Your heart and your talent are planet-sized. Kathryn Harrison, thank you for teaching me the importance of artistic risk. Louise DeSalvo, beloved teacher, mentor, and friend, thank you for believing in me when I did not believe in myself. Professor Michael Dowdy, thank you for telling me Pittsburgh needed to be written about. Jan Heller Levi, I'm so grateful for the opportunity you gave me to study alongside you.

Bruce and Geneva Boyd, thank you for being such treasured friends and for inspiring me daily. Anna Philip, thank you for showing me what it means to be brave. To the real-life Layne and Aria, what would I do without your steadfast friendship? I am a better person because of it. To my brother and sister, thank you for making me laugh and for always welcoming me home. To my parents, thank you for loving me with every ounce of your hearts. If I ever have half your integrity and your spirit, I will count myself incredibly lucky. I am honored to be your daughter. And Rajan, thank you for always being the best part of my day. My life became infinitely better the moment you walked into it.